The Day the Whores Came Out to Play Tennis and Other Plays

Also by *Arthur Kopit*

OH DAD, POOR DAD,
MAMMA'S HUNG YOU IN THE CLOSET
AND I'M FEELIN' SO SAD

INDIANS

The Day the Whores Came Out to Play Tennis and Other Plays

by

ARTHUR KOPIT

❧

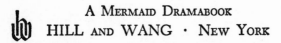
A MERMAID DRAMABOOK

HILL AND WANG · NEW YORK

FIRST DRAMABOOK PRINTING MARCH 1965

Thirteenth printing, 1979

To my Parents

CONTENTS

INTRODUCTION

THE PLAYS included in this volume were written over a period of seven and a half years; therefore a few words regarding them and their chronology might be helpful.

"The Questioning of Nick" is the first play I ever wrote and is included, not because of that fact but because, on re-reading it for the first time in many years, I found myself not altogether displeased with its effect—a somewhat negative sounding comment I know, but since my usual reaction when re-reading things I have written is sadness at not having thrown them out it seemed a positive reaction indeed. I am especially pleased with its inclusion however because it is, up till now, the only realistic play I have written. So, for those people who say to me, "But when are you going to write a *real* play?"—here it is. (I assume, when they say real, that what they mean is realistic. I hope I am not wrong.) As for its background, I wrote it during spring vacation of my sophomore year at Harvard. Gaynor Bradish, who was a tutor in Dunster House at that time and in charge of its excellent Drama Workshop, had urged his students to write one-act plays for performance in the Workshop that spring. "The Questioning of Nick" was the result of that suggestion. The next fall it won a college-wide playwrighting contest and was performed on a more public scale. My career was determined. (At least, that is, in my mind.)

A year later "Sing to Me Through Open Windows" was written and produced. Unlike "The Questioning of Nick," which has never been rewritten, "Sing to Me" has been extensively and frequently rewritten ever since. It is hoped that by its publication I will at last be forced to leave the play alone. I should also say that in 1962 it was performed in previews in New York as a curtain raiser to *Oh Dad, Poor Dad, Mamma's Hung You in the Closet and I'm Feelin' So Sad*. Unfortunately (for the production as staged by Jerome Robbins was wonderful), the play had to be cancelled before its opening night since the set change between plays, due to the limited backstage space of the Phoenix Theatre, could not be accomplished in less than thirty minutes and the audience, when it finally returned to its seats from this extraordinary intermission, was thoroughly worn out.

The next play in the present volume to be written was "Chamber Music." The idea for it came, I think, some time in 1959. It was not begun however until the late spring of 1962. It was finished that summer. In the winter of 1963 "Chamber Music" was performed in previews in New York with another one-act play of mine, the entire program being called *Asylum*. These plays also were cancelled before opening night, this time however because I wanted to do more work on them. This past summer "Chamber Music" was revised and rewritten. Its companion play will be expanded into a three-act play sometime in, I hope, the near future.

"The Day the Whores Came Out to Play Tennis" came next. It was written in the fall and winter of 1963-64 and rewritten in the early summer.

"The Conquest of Everest" and "The Hero" were both written in 1964 on a pleasant March weekend. "The Hero" has no dialogue because I was struck dumb by the prospect of writing two plays in a single day.

ARTHUR KOPIT

New York City
November 12, 1964

CHAMBER MUSIC

A Play in One Act

CHARACTERS

Woman Who Plays Records
Woman in Safari Outfit
Woman with Notebook
Girl in Gossamer Dress
Woman in aviatrix's Outfit
Woman in Queenly Spanish Garb
Woman in Armor
Woman with Gavel
Man in White
His Assistant

Scene—A meeting room.

CHAMBER MUSIC

The lights have not come up yet. If there is a curtain, it is
still drawn. Heard vaguely in the distance: the Allegro
moderato from Mozart's Quartet in F Major (K. 590).
Then the lights come up. We are in a room with a large
horseshoe-shaped table in the center. Around the table are
eight chairs. The only other thing in the room is an old
portable phonograph resting on a small table or stool.

At the start a chunky, carelessly dressed WOMAN *is seen*
by the phonograph. She turns it off. The Mozart ceases.
She takes the record off, walks over to a window, opens it
and stares far out. Looking up at the sky now, she cups
her hand to her ear. But, alas, hearing nothing, she lowers
her hand and walks sadly away. She hugs the record in
her arms. The door opens and a WOMAN IN A SAFARI
OUTFIT *enters. She wears a pith helmet draped with*
mosquito netting. The netting is covering her face. She
carries a toy rifle.

WOMAN IN SAFARI OUTFIT. Was that you, just now?

Woman Who Plays Records. Vat?

Woman in Safari Outfit. I said, "Was that you?" Just
now? *Making all that racket?*

Woman Who Plays Records. Racket? Vat means by a
racket, hm? Vat means by a *"racket"*?

And, so saying, the WOMAN WHO PLAYS RECORDS *turns*
sharply away, hiding her record at the same time. The
WOMAN IN SAFARI OUTFIT *glares at her.*

Woman in Safari Outfit. Goddamn mosquitoes. [*She*
takes off her pith helmet and picks at the netting. Proudly
she holds something up in display.] Aha!

Woman Who Plays Records. Vat?

Woman in Safari Outfit. Anopheles quadrimaculatus.
You can tell by the jaw structure. [*The* WOMAN WHO
PLAYS RECORDS *peers closely. It is obvious that she can't*
see a thing.] Well, close that window! You want 'em to
eat us *alive?*

3

The WOMAN WHO PLAYS RECORDS *rushes over to the window and closes it.*

Woman Who Plays Records. Can't imagine vy it vas open in the first place. [*She giggles.*]

The WOMAN IN SAFARI OUTFIT *finds her place card at the table and sits. She mashes the supposed mosquito on the table. She examines its entrails. Through the open door now two women enter. The first is short and stout and carries a notebook. The second is frail, looks rather frightened, and wears a gossamer dress.*

Woman with Notebook. Ramon Navarro collected Renaissance p-paintings. Were you aware of that? [*The* GIRL IN GOSSAMER DRESS *smiles with innocence.*] And yet you say you were in the movies. [*The* GIRL IN GOSSAMER DRESS *takes the first seat she comes to. The* WOMAN WITH NOTEBOOK *stares at the* WOMAN IN SAFARI OUTFIT.] What's wrong? F-flaw in the fu-furniture?

Woman in Safari Outfit. No. Mosquito.

Woman Who Plays Records. Dey jus' don' make furniture de vay dey used to. No sirree.

Woman with Notebook [*to the* WOMAN WHO PLAYS RECORDS]. Your husband is not as good as B-B-B-Beethoven.

Woman Who Plays Records [*in terror*]. Vat?

The WOMAN WITH NOTEBOOK *roars with laughter. She finds her seat and sits, as the* WOMAN IN AVIATRIX'S OUTFIT *enters.*

Girl in Gossamer Dress. Hi!

The WOMAN IN AVIATRIX'S OUTFIT *goes over to the* GIRL IN GOSSAMER DRESS, *leans over her shoulder, and examines the place card.*

Woman in Aviatrix's Outfit. That card has *my* name on it.

The GIRL IN GOSSAMER DRESS *jumps up and takes another seat.*

Woman with Notebook. Actually, I don't think he's as good as H-Haydn, either.

Woman Who Plays Records [*to the* WOMAN IN AVA-TRIX'S OUTFIT]. Hidin'? Who's hidin'? Hidin' from vat?

Woman in Aviatrix's Outfit. Joseph Haydn was a composer. Miss Stein is trying to say that *she* feels he's a better composer than Mozart.

Woman Who Plays Records. Vat?

The WOMAN WITH NOTEBOOK *roars with laughter again, as the* WOMAN IN QUEENLY SPANISH GARB *enters. The* GIRL IN GOSSAMER DRESS *jumps up and rushes over to a certain chair, checks the place card, pulls out the chair. The* SPANISH QUEEN *sits. The* GIRL IN GOSSAMER DRESS *returns to her own seat—or supposedly the right seat, for in checking the place card she discovers that an error has again been made. So again she jumps up and finds her proper place. She giggles.*

Woman in Aviatrix's Outfit. Why do you always hold the chair for her?

Girl in Gossamer Dress. Hm?

Woman in Aviatrix's Outfit. At our meetings you always hold the chair for her. Why? You're as good as she is.

Girl in Gossamer Dress. No, I'm not. *She* is a queen.

A beam of wood now enters through the door. At its far end, supporting it at its crossbar, is a WOMAN IN ARMOR. *There is a crucifix on her breastplate. Evidently what she is carrying is simply another crucifix. Only the one she is carrying is well over seven feet long. In attempting to enter the room the crossbar of the crucifix slams into the doorframe and catches fast.*

Woman in Armor. Oh, shit. Well, for chrissakes one of you *help* me with this thing!

The WOMAN WHO PLAYS RECORDS *rushes to the door and begins, with frantic and totally contradictory hand signals, to guide the crucifix into the room.*

Woman Who Plays Records. All right now, a little to the right. Oi-yoi-yoi, povolie! *Povolie!*

Woman in Safari Outfit. I'm gonna take that goddamn piece of wood someday and break it, I swear! What right has she got dragging it like that into other people's rooms? What *right* has she got?

Girl in Gossamer Dress. This isn't your room.

Woman in Safari Outfit. What?

Girl in Gossamer Dress. Well, I was only——

Woman in Safari Outfit [*turning sharply to the* WOMAN WITH NOTEBOOK]. D'you think this is right?

Woman with Notebook. Well——

Woman Who Plays Records [*directing all the time*]. Now. A biss'l der zeit.

Woman with Notebook. It *does* tend to tend to tend to——

Woman Who Plays Records [*coaxing the crucifix in with "body English"*]. Oo-oo-oo-oo.

Woman with Notebook. Create a problem of s-s-s-space.

Woman in Safari Outfit. You bet your big cookies it does.

Girl in Gossamer Dress. What I *meant* to say was: it's as much her room as it is yours.

Woman in Safari Outfit. Aghhh!

Woman Who Plays Records [*as the crucifix slips through the door*]. Oi, dienken Gott. You made it.

Woman in Armor [*pushing back the visor of her helmet*]. In the name of King Charles the Seventh, and with special mention for Catherine, Margaret, and Michael, without whose assistance this could not be possible, I honor you for the nobility and selflessness of your act.

Woman Who Plays Records. T'ank you.

Woman in Armor [*brightly*]. Well, now. Where to put it!

Woman in Safari Outfit [*under her breath*]. *I'll* tell her where to——

Woman in Aviatrix's Outfit. Down! [*The* WOMAN IN ARMOR, *the crucifix balanced on her shoulder, has swung about. Just in time the ladies duck and thus avoid decapitation. Cautiously they sit back up.*] Again!

The WOMAN IN ARMOR, *having found no place suitable for her crucifix, has turned back. In doing so, the crucifix,*

*like a deadly pendulum, has retraced its arc. Once again
the ladies duck just in time.*

Woman in Armor. Sorry. [*Whereupon she promptly
lowers—or, more accurately, drops—the enormous object
on the table. Again the ladies scatter in time.*] Uh . . .
sorry.

And the ladies take their seats, a bit shaken by it all.

Woman in Aviatrix's Outfit. And yet she wonders why
she's never invited anywhere.

Woman in Armor. I *said* I was sorry.

Woman in Safari Outfit. It's suicide with her around.
Nothing less.

Girl in Gossamer Dress. Twice it's hit me on the head.

Woman in Armor. Look, I *said* I was sorry, didn't I?

Woman in Safari Outfit. Honey, I'll tell you something.
If you haven't gotten rid of that overgrown machete of
yours by tomorrow, I'm gonna personally take it and wrap
it, like a scarf, around your goddamn neck!

Woman with Notebook. Well put.

Woman in Armor [*pouting*]. I said I was sorry.

Girl in Gossamer Dress [*to the* WOMAN IN SAFARI OUT-
FIT]. You know, *twice* it's hit me on the head.

Woman in Safari Outfit. Aghhh, she's out of her mind.

Woman Who Plays Records. Joan, you know I vouldn't
tell a lie. So believe me, de t'ing is *enormous*. Better off
you left it somevere else.

Woman in Armor. No.

Woman Who Plays Records [*to the others*]. Maybe if
ve got her a smaller vun?

Woman in Armor. No! [*And she slams her visor shut.*]

Girl in Gossamer Dress [*to the* WOMAN IN SAFARI OUT-
FIT]. Twice already it's hit me on the head. And *hard*,
too.

Woman in Safari Outfit [*getting annoyed with the* GIRL
IN GOSSAMER DRESS]. Well, what d'you *expect*? She's out
of her *cotton-pickin'* mind!

Woman Who Plays Records [*talking through the visor
as if it were a telephone*]. Joanie, dear, listen to me. . . .

Joanie? [*When there's no response she peers in through the slats. To the others, in a whisper.*] You know vhat? I don't t'ink she's in dere.

Woman in Safari Outfit [*to the woman nearest her, motioning toward the* WOMAN WHO PLAYS RECORDS]. Now you know why they're friends. [*She gets up and goes over to the* WOMAN IN ARMOR. *She opens her visor.*] Honey, it's only a piece of *wood!*

Woman in Armor [*pouting*]. Don't care. [*And again she snaps her visor shut.*]

Woman in Safari Outfit. Agh! [*To the others.*] If it weren't for the fact that I'd bust my hand, I *swear* I'd hit her! Right in the goddamned face.

Woman in Aviatrix's Outfit. Joan, darling. Listen to me for a second.

The WOMAN WHO PLAYS RECORDS *opens the* WOMAN IN ARMOR's *visor.*

Woman Who Plays Records. Joanie, dear, be a nice girl for a minute and listen to Amelia. She's got something *very important* to say. [*To the* WOMAN IN AVIATRIX'S OUTFIT.] All right. Go ahead.

Woman in Aviatrix's Outfit. Joan——

Woman in Armor. No! I'll *never* give it away!

Woman in Aviatrix's Outfit. Not give it away, honey. *Put* it away. In storage. No one's going to take the thing.

Girl in Gossamer Dress [*to the* WOMAN IN ARMOR]. *Twice* it's hit me on the head. Right here. And hard, too.

Woman Who Plays Records. Believe me, Joan, it's a very dangerous t'ing you've got dere ven you don't handle it right. It's a veapon. An absolute *veapon.*

Woman in Armor. Don't care. It came with the armor. So it stays with me. It's mine. And you *can't have it!*

Woman in Aviatrix's Outfit. Joan——

Woman in Armor. Nor can you tell me what to do. So. Hah! Hah! Hah!

Whereupon the WOMAN IN ARMOR *slams her visor shut and thus ends that. Short stunned pause.*

Woman Who Plays Records. I donno. I jus' donno. To

me it's vun t'ing dat she's out of her mind. But does she have to be such an idiot as vell?

At which point the WOMAN WITH NOTEBOOK *laughs wildly. Everyone turns to her in amazement. But as soon as they do, she is as quiet and unsmiling as before. It is almost as if she were not aware she had laughed at all in that brief and mad split second.*

Enter a tall, severely dressed WOMAN WITH A GAVEL *in her hand.*

Woman with Gavel. Afternoon, ladies. [*She closes the door behind her.*] Sorry I'm late. [*She walks over to the table and takes her seat at its head.*] I think perhaps we should draw the shades. [*A few of the women rush over to the windows and draw the shades.*] Also, check the door. [*One of the women checks the door.*] It is my pleasure then to announce that the Sixth Annual Meeting of the Duly-Elected Grievance and Someday-Governing Committee of Wing Five, Women's Section——

Woman Who Plays Records. He-ah he-ah for the Vomen's Section!

All [*except the* WOMAN WITH GAVEL, *the* WOMAN IN QUEENLY SPANISH GARB, *and the* WOMAN IN AVIATRIX'S OUTFIT]. Hip-hip——

Woman Who Plays Records. Hooray!

All. Hip——

The WOMAN WITH GAVEL *brings silence with a sharp rap.*

Woman with Gavel. . . . may now *hopefully* commence. The secretary will read the minutes of our last meeting. Trudy? *If you please.*

Woman with Notebook [*reading from her notebook*]. "The meeting was called to order at the usual time all being present for the meeting which was called to order at the usual time in order those meeting at the usual time in order to meet at the usual time might meet at the usual time and thus be meeting then and be a meeting then and a usual one, too. And thus the meeting, having been called to order at the usual time, all being present for the meeting which——" [*A loud yawn is*

heard coming from the WOMAN IN ARMOR. *The secretary
stops reading at once.*]

> Joan of Arc
> Died in the dark!

Woman in Armor.

> Gertrude Stein
> Can't write a line!

*Giggles from some of the girls. The president raps her
gavel. Order returns.*

Woman with Notebook. "The meeting was called to
order at the——" [*Again a yawn from the* WOMAN IN
ARMOR. *More giggling from the girls.*] *Madame President . . .*

Woman with Gavel. Minutes approved.

Woman with Notebook [*as the women all cheer*]. What!

Girl in Gossamer Dress. Well, after all, there *are* more
important things for us to discuss than your silly minutes

Woman in Safari Outfit. You tell her, honey.

Woman with Notebook. Ob-ob-ob-*jection!*

Woman in Armor.

> Gertrude Stein
> Looks like a swine.

Woman with Notebook [*helplessly*]. Madame President . . .

The women roar with laughter.

Woman in Safari Outfit. Just wasting time. Just wasting
our good ol' time.

Woman with Gavel. Ladies, *please!*

The laughter stops.

Woman in Safari Outfit. Imagine, *Anopheles quadrimaculatus.* You know they've given the Nobel for less
than this. [*She snaps a picture of the table.*]

Woman with Notebook. "The meeting was——"

Woman with Gavel. They've been *approved.*

Woman in Armor [*sotto voce*].

> Gertrude Stein
> Is doing fine.

Girl in Gossamer Dress [*waving a slip of paper*]. I have here, in my possession, the record of——

Woman with Gavel. And as for *you*, Pearl White, we'll get to you in good time. [*In an aside to the* WOMAN WITH NOTEBOOK.] *Movie stars!*

Woman with Notebook. "The meeting was——"

Woman with Gavel. They've been *approved!* [*The* WOMAN WITH NOTEBOOK *raises her hand.*] Miss Stein.

Woman with Notebook. I move that the p-president be im-m-m-m-m-peached.

Giggling from the others.

Woman with Gavel. Any seconds? [*The giggling stops.*] Motion shelved.

Woman in Armor.

Gertrude Stein
Is doing fine.

Woman with Notebook.

Joan of Arc
Died in the dark!

Woman with Gavel. Miss Earhart? The floor is yours.

Woman with Notebook. Oh Susan B. Anthony, Susan B. Anthony, *who* is Susan B. Anthony that she can rap-raprap her gavel and have women be like men, that is quiet? . . . Rapraprap. Rap. Rap. Rap.

The WOMAN WITH NOTEBOOK *closes her notebook. Long pause. And then the* GIRL IN GOSSAMER DRESS *rises and walks to a window, throws open the shades, and stares out. A moment later she turns back and faces the others. She closes the curtains behind her.*

Girl in Gossamer Dress [*distantly*]. No. Not there. I guess they're still hiding. . . . The sun has fallen again.

The GIRL IN GOSSAMER DRESS *walks back to her chair and sits. Silence for a time. And then the* WOMAN IN AVIATRIX'S OUTFIT *rises.*

Woman in Aviatrix's Outfit. I . . . am Amelia Earhart. That is to say, I *am* Amelia Earhart. And I want to get out of here. One of the main reasons for this is the fact that

I'm not insane. In fact, I'm not even exceptionally neu-
rotic. I'm simply Amelia Earhart and I want to get the
hell out.

Woman in Safari Outfit. Where you wanna go, honey?
The South Seas?

General laughter.

Woman in Aviatrix's Outfit. I am growing *old* in here!

Woman Who Plays Records. Darling, *none* of us are
growing younger.

General laughter.

Woman in Aviatrix's Outfit. All right, check the records if you like. It's all down there; I'm not lying. July
second, 1937. That's the day I crashed. Right out there in
the yard. July second, 1937. Go on, check the records if
you like. Why should I lie? [*Loud laughter from the
others.*] Look, my plane is still there. Isn't *that* proof
enough? [*General laughter.*] Well, true, they've turned it
into a playground for lost children. True, it's not the plane
it used to be. The valiant, gallant plane it used to be. But
still, that shouldn't matter. The *shape* of it should be proof
enough. Well, if you don't believe me ask Fred Noonan!
Ask my trusted friend and pilot, Frederick the Great
Noonan! Over there, behind those formidable walls, they've
got *him* prisoner, too! Well, go on if you don't believe me.
Send someone over and ask him. Ask him what my name
is, and where I used to live so long ago. Ask him if what
I say isn't true! [*Uproarious laughter.*] Stop laughing! Stop
laughing! Stop! [*She holds her ears. They stop.*] I really
am telling you the truth, you see. I really *am* Amelia
Earhart. [*Short pause.*] And I'm growing old in here. . . .
[*The laughter builds madly.*] Stop *laughing at me!* Stop
laughing at me! *Stop laughing* . . .

Woman with Notebook. Are are we are we to to assume
are we to assume that Miss that Miss Earhart would have
us have us would have us believe that Miss Earhart would
have us believe that we are not-not-not whom we *think*
we are?

Woman in Aviatrix's Outfit. But I *am* Amelia Earhart

That's the terrible thing, you see . . . I truly am. [*And she sits sadly in her chair.*]

Woman in Armor. Then who am I? Charles the Seventh?

Woman with Notebook. And and who am I? F. Scott Fitzg-g-gerald?

Girl in Gossamer Dress. D. W. Griffith?

Woman in Safari Outfit. Stanley and Livingston?

Woman with Gavel. Abraham Lincoln?

Woman Who Plays Records. Mrs. Johann Sebastian Bach?

Girl in Gossamer Dress. And if all that's so, who is she if not beautiful Isabella of ancient Spain?

Woman in Safari Outfit. Christopher Columbus, maybe?

Girl in Gossamer Dress. Yes, who is she? *Who is she?*

Short pause.

Woman in Aviatrix's Outfit. I don't know.

Pause.

Woman with Notebook.

Amelia Earhart
Is a dear-heart.

The WOMAN IN SAFARI OUTFIT *has raised her hand.*

Woman with Gavel. The chair recognizes that noted hunter Osa Johnson.

Woman in Safari Outfit. Explorer, honey.

Woman with Gavel. I . . . *meant* explorer.

Woman in Safari Outfit. Yeah. Um, I've got a letter here from Mrs. Neoceballrus in Room Eighty-two. She says——

Woman in Armor. We know what she says. She says it every year!

Woman in Safari Outfit. But——

Woman with Notebook.

Mrs. Neoceballrus
Looks like a walrus.

Woman with Gavel. I really don't think, Mrs. Johnson, that it's necessary for us to go into this matter again. And I say that only because to discuss her problem would be, in effect, to do nothing but waste our time. To quote, if I may from memory, Mrs. Neoceballrus: "The dilemma of my life is that I'm convinced I've never been born." Well. As we all know, not two months ago there was obtained, through the efforts of this committee and a certain hand-some young doctor, a bona fide birth certificate proving, beyond the shadow of a doubt that Mrs. Neoceballrus had, in fact, *already* been born. Now, of course, it's pos-sible that she may want more proof. But that, I think, is a little pushy. One birth should be enough for anyone. And since she's already had it, *I* say: the lady has no more problems.

Woman in Aviatrix's Outfit. Except, of course, that she's stark, raving mad.

Whereupon everyone turns slowly and stares at the aviatrix.

Long, cold pause.

Woman in Armor. Madame President.

Woman with Gavel [*turning her gaze from the* WOMAN IN AVIATRIX'S OUTFIT]. The chair recognizes Joan of Arc.

Woman with Notebook [*sotto voce*].

Joan of Arc
Died in the dark.
She laughs hysterically.

Woman in Armor. Gertrude Stein is *fat! That's* why she looks like a swine!

The WOMAN WITH NOTEBOOK *stops laughing.*

Woman with Gavel. The chair recognizes Joan of Arc!

Woman in Armor. Well, here is the problem. What's to be done about my voices? They are . . . *bothering me.*

Girl in Gossamer Dress [*hesitantly*]. Ob . . . objection. [*And then she rises nervously.*] Um, *I* think—well, I don't actually know much about these things, you understand. [*She giggles.*] So I suppose I shouldn't talk.

Woman in Safari Outfit. On with it, honey!

Girl in Gossamer Dress. Well. I think . . . um, that this is just the sort of thing the committee can't help with. That is, to me it's the sort of thing you must, well, some-how . . . work out for yourself. That's all.

The GIRL IN GOSSAMER DRESS *sits bashfully. The* WOMAN IN ARMOR *takes off her helmet for the first time.*

Woman in Armor. But, you see, I didn't *expect* help. I . . . don't think I really even wanted it. I, well, just would have appreciated some . . . you know, *guidance* in the matter. . . .

Woman with Notebook [*sotto voce*].
Joan of Arc
Died in the dark.
Joan of Arc
Died in the dark. . . .
Joan of Arc,
Died in the dark.

The WOMAN IN ARMOR *turns and stares at the* WOMAN WITH NOTEBOOK. *Then, after a moment—and almost without expression—she puts her helmet back on. She sits. The* WOMAN WITH NOTEBOOK *continues to laugh, softly. The laughter grows more distant. No one moves. . . . And then slowly, unnoticed by anyone, the* WOMAN WHO PLAYS RECORDS *rises, crosses to the phonograph, switches it on, takes a record out of hiding, puts it on, and rushes to the window as the last part of Donna Anna's last aria from* Don Giovanni *begins. She pulls open the drapes and throws open the window. Still no one seems to notice.*

Donna Anna (*on the record*). . . . *non vuoi ch'io mora.* [*The* WOMAN WHO PLAYS RECORDS *moves her lips to match the words as if she were singing them.*]
Non mi dir, bell' idol mio,
Che son io crudel con te.
Calma, calma il tuo tormento,
Se di duol non vuoi ch'io mora.
Non vuoi ch'io mora.

It is the orchestra's turn now and the WOMAN WHO PLAYS RECORDS *rubs her hands in nervous anticipation of the aria's end. But meanwhile the other women have become aware of the event happening and, having become aware, have risen en masse and gone to the phonograph.*

The WOMAN WITH GAVEL *reaches down into the machine.*
        Forse un giorno——

[*And the* WOMAN WITH GAVEL *lifts the record off the machine, a cold smile on her face.*]

WOMAN WHO PLAYS RECORDS. No-o-o-o-o-o-o! [*The* WOMAN WITH GAVEL *cracks the record. The women start toward the* WOMAN WHO PLAYS RECORDS. *She backs away. They continue to pursue her. She starts now to sing as she runs. It is obviously the first time she has ever had the nerve to sing alone. Her voice, to say the least, is dreadful.*]

        Forse un giorno il cielo ancora
        Sentirà pietà di me.

[*Pursued, no place left to go, she climbs up on the table.*]
        Sentirà . . .

And then, bravely, the WOMAN WHO PLAYS RECORDS *begins to croak the coloratura cadenza as the women reach up and drag her down—though it is to her credit that she fights to the end, struggling always to have her voice heard, to finish the aria somehow. Suddenly all the others rush to their seats and sit in mock innocence. The* WOMAN WHO PLAYS RECORDS *weeps silently, her face buried in her hands. The door opens. The* MAN *enters, a white coat on. Behind him is his* ASSISTANT.

Man in White [*brightly*]. Well! How are all my lovely ladies on this fine day? Getting along well, I trust? [*He goes to the window and closes it.*] Must keep the windows closed, girls. I've told you that. And many times. Yes, many times.

Meanwhile the ASSISTANT *has gone over to the phonograph. He notices the broken record all over the floor.*
        Assistant. Sir.

The MAN IN WHITE *walks over and stares at the record bits. Then he reaches down and shuts off the phonograph. He stares at it. The ladies giggle. He walks over to the* WOMAN WHO PLAYS RECORDS *and gives her the broken pieces*

Man in White Come on now, chins up, all three of

them. Tha-a-at's the way. Now. Where's that lovely, girl-
ish smile? O-o-o-oh, not the itty-bitty smile. I mean the
big, *big* smile. Ahhhh, there. Now. You see? *All-l-l better.*
[*When he chucks her under her chin, however, her smile
disappears, though he does not see this. He walks now
over to the* WOMAN WITH GAVEL *and, standing behind
her, his hands on her shoulders, addresses the other ladies.*]
Well now, just what do you suppose I'm going to say?
Well, *this* is what I'm going to say: if you nice ladies
don't behave yourselves, you'll never have another meeting. And do you know what that means? Well, for one,
it means you'll never again be allowed to make suggestions to us about things you think should be done, or
improved, or looked after. And it also means that all the
lovely ladies who elected you to this nice committee and
placed in you all their hope and trust, yes, it means all
those lovely ladies will then hate you. Forever. [*He smiles
broadly.*] Well now! Having said my little piece, I think
it time you got back to your little meeting. I bet there must
be just all *sorts* of fine things you've set your hearts on
accomplishing today. [*He opens the* WOMAN IN ARMOR'S
visor and peers in.] Hello. Not too stuffy in there for you,
is it? [*She snaps her visor shut. He gets his finger out of
the way just in time. He chuckles. To all, in leaving.*] Ah,
well. Carry on. And remember: "decorum" is the word.
Spell it as it sounds. [*And, nodding to his companion,
they leave the room.*]

*Silence at the table. Everyone stares blankly ahead. After
a while the* WOMAN IN SAFARI OUTFIT *takes out a pack
of cigarettes.*

Woman in Safari Outfit [*to the lady on her left*].
Cigarette?

Lady on Her Left. Thanks. [*To the lady on her left.*]
Cigarette?

Lady on Her Left [*taking one and then offering one to
the lady on her left*]. Cigarette?

Lady on Her Left. Thanks. [*And then she offers one to
the lady on her left.*] Cigarette?

Lady on Her *Left.* Thanks. [*She offers one to the lady on* her *left.*]

Lady on Her *Left.* Thanks. [*To the lady on* her *left— the Spanish lady.*] Cigarette?

The WOMAN IN QUEENLY SPANISH GARB *takes one without comment and offers one to the lady on* her *left.*

The Lady on Her *Left.* Thanks. [*And she returns the pack to the* WOMAN IN SAFARI OUTFIT.]

They all puff away nervously. Since, however, they do not have matches they do not light the cigarettes. They keep puffing. Pause.

Woman in Safari Outfit. In Borneo they'd never heard of Barrymore or Calvin Coolidge. Martin showed 'em movies. One day the projector broke. That was when they ate our cameraman. I don't think that was very nice.

Girl in Gossamer Dress. I was browsing through *Mechanics Illustrated* the other day.

Woman in Armor. My pants are getting rusty.

Girl in Gossamer Dress. It said the French——

Woman in Armor The who?

Girl in Gossamer Dress. The French.

Woman in Armor. Oh. Don't like the French.

Girl in Gossamer Dress. It said the French——

Woman in Armor. They let me down, they did.

Girl in Gossamer Dress. It said the French——

Woman in Armor. No. Don't like the French.

Girl in Gossamer Dress. Well, it said the French have built this train that travels ninety miles an hour. Now steam locomotives—or "Puffing Billies," as we used to call them—they only went twenty. Ninety's much faster. Doesn't leave a person nearly enough time. Why there I'd be, flat on the tracks and just beginning to slip out of the ropes when clickety-clack—— No. Things are just too dangerous nowadays. I'll stay right here, if you don't mind.

Woman in Armor. My pants are getting rusty.

Woman with Notebook. A riddle: if Pablo still ate

Pablum and Ernest were more honest, would Alice still feel malice? That's the riddle. That is my riddle.

Woman Who Plays Records. Oi, to be married to Mozart. Oi-yoi-yoi, vat a life dat is to live. A man like dat. Imagine. A genius. A god. And *my* husband. *All* at de same time! Vell, I'll tell you, de're not *many* vomen in de neighborhood as lucky as dat!

Woman in Safari Outfit. Sometimes, during festivals, the natives would eat their friends. We were told this was an honor. But Martin and I, we just never made friends easily. That's the way it was with us.

Woman in Armor. And while we're at it, what's to be done about my voices? Yes. Tell me that.

Woman with Gavel.

> Oh, I loved Elizabeth Cady,
> And Elizabeth Cady loved me.
> And when she was nearly eighty,
> Sweet Cady, she still loved me.

Woman in Armor. The hell with my voices! What's to be done about my pants?

Woman with Notebook. Susan B. Anthony. *Who* is Susan B. Anthony? Who *is* Susan B. Anthony? *Who-is-Susan-B.-Anthony?*

Woman with Gavel. "The right to sleep is given to no woman." You gave me those lines, Trudy. In *The Mother of Us All.* A marvelous play, I think. "The right to sleep is given to no woman." Yes. Yes, Trudy. How pertinent those lines are, even today.

Pause.

Woman in Aviatrix's Outfit. Yes, ask Fred if you don't believe me. Ask Fred Noonan. Captured during the course of a crash. His Amelia was a really good pilot. Not much of a navigator. But a really good pilot. You just ask Fred.

Pause.

Woman in Safari Outfit. I hate—— Agh! [*She snubs out her cigarette violently.*] What I hate is, I hate cigarettes without *matches!* That's what I hate! It's so . . . so . . .

Woman Who Plays Records. You're absolutely right, darling. Smoking's just not de same ven you can't have smoke.

The GIRL IN GOSSAMER DRESS *moans.*

Woman in Armor [*with a nervous laugh*]. One of the main troubles with a suit of armor which one rarely thinks of is: it's very hard to tiptoe around in. Just . . . thought I'd mention it. Don't . . . know why.

Nervous laughter from the others.

Woman in Safari Outfit [*with fury toward* WOMAN IN ARMOR]. I'm gonna break that goddamn piece of——

The WOMAN IN SAFARI OUTFIT *goes for the crucifix. The* WOMAN IN ARMOR *leaps up and blocks her way. The two women square off. Pause. At last, having thought better of picking a fight with the* WOMAN IN ARMOR, *the* WOMAN IN SAFARI OUTFIT *goes back and sits down. As for the* WOMAN IN ARMOR, *she sits too, but clutching the crucifix like a child to her breast. She sobs softly, stroking the wood.*

Girl in Gossamer Dress. Yes, I think I'll stay right here, if you don't mind. Yes. Right here is home enough for me.

Woman with Notebook. Who is Susan B. Anthony? Who is she, Susan B. Anthony? Who is she . . . ?

Silence. The WOMAN WITH GAVEL *looks down at the table. She stares at her gavel. She picks it up. She looks at it. Long pause. Then she looks up at all the women.*

Woman with Gavel. Well. Out with the old business. In with the new.

The GIRL IN GOSSAMER DRESS *rises.*

Girl in Gossamer Dress. I have here the record of hostile occurrences kept, as requested by our president, Miss Anthony. January fourth, eight fifteen A.M., Miss Marianne Sweetumback of Room Seven Twenty-one reports definite sensations of be-lli-ger-*ency?*

Woman with Gavel. Belligerency.

Girl in Gossamer Dress. Belligerency directed ⁺oward

her while sitting at the breakfast table eating her thirty-second bowl of porridge. As a result re-gur- . . .

Woman with Gavel. Vomits.

Girl in Gossamer Dress. Vomits into it. When asked who was sitting with her at the time, she replies only the cook. Conclusion. Source of—— Oh, God.

Woman with Gavel. Belliger——

Girl in Gossamer Dress. Belligerency unknown. February twelfth, three twenty-one P.M. While singing something called a madrigal. *Madrigal?*

Woman with Gavel. Madrigal.

Girl in Gossamer Dress. Madrigal. . . . What's a madrigal?

Woman with Gavel. Go on with your report.

Girl in Gossamer Dress. Madrigal for the Music Appreciation Society of Ward Six, Mrs. McGraw and Mrs. McBurner report definite feelings of homicide—— That's murder!

Woman with Gavel. That's right.

Girl in Gossamer Dress. Directed toward them. As a result, cease singing at once. Ho-mi-cidal feeling later verified—— *Verified?*

Woman with Gavel. Validated. [*No help to Pearl.*] Go on with your report.

Girl in Gossamer Dress. By their accompanist . . .

Woman in Safari Outfit. Piano player, honey!

Girl in Gossamer Dress. Miss McFactin. Though strangely enough, denied by those ladies of the Music Appreciation Society who happened, at that moment, to be sitting in the room. *What's a madrigal?* [*The* WOMAN WITH GAVEL *glares at her.*] April third, sometime around noon. Miss Amanda d'Workenwick Alston-Cartwright of Suite Eight Twenty-three, Eight Twenty-four, Eight Twenty-five, and Eight Twenty-six reports definite sensations of hostility—— I know what *that* is!

Woman in Safari Outfit. You bet your sweet ass you do.

The WOMAN WITH GAVEL *raps her gavel.*

Girl in Gossamer Dress. Definite sensations of hostility

directed toward her while collecting money for her annual Whitsuntide pageant. Miss Alston-Cartwright rightly concludes that since Whitsuntide is a religious event, this hostility could not have emanated from any of the women she'd solicited money from. Which was, as usual, everyone in the ward.

Woman Who Plays Records. Yeah. And it left me vithout a penny.

Woman in Safari Outfit. Not as bad, honey, as whatever it was that left you without a *brain.*

Giggling from the girls, WOMAN WHO PLAYS RECORDS *included. The* WOMAN WITH GAVEL *raps for silence.*

Girl in Gossamer Dress. In short, then, these reports all prove that no source can be found for the various feelings of hatred, hostility, jealousy, be-lli-gerency [*giggles*] and revenge known to exist. The conclusion then. The source must come from *outside* our ward. Or, in other words, the *Men's* Ward! Which none of us have ever seen. And is therefore, most likely.

Woman with Gavel. Pearl, a good report.

Woman with Notebook. I h-h-helped her with it.

Girl in Gossamer Dress. You did *not!*

Woman with Gavel [*rapping her gavel*]. Ladies!

Woman in Armor [*sotto voce*].

> Gertrude Stein
> Drank too much wine.

Rap of gavel. The WOMAN IN ARMOR *quiet.*

Woman Who Plays Records. Vat I vanna know is, why didn't ve get to de report sooner? After all, you know, it's vat ve're really here for. I mean, to save our lives.

Girl in Gossamer Dress. Before they attack!

Woman with Notebook. Which could be any m-m-minute.

Woman in Safari Outfit. But most likely will occur at night.

Woman in Armor. The dead of night.

Woman in Aviatrix's Outfit. Yes, just incredible.

Woman with Gavel [*sharply*]. I beg your pardon?

Woman in Aviatrix's Outfit. I said it's *just incredible.*

Woman with Gavel. What's incredible?

Woman in Aviatrix's Outfit. All this nonsense . . .

Everyone turns and stares at her with cold hatred. Pause.

Woman with Gavel [*having regained her briefly lost composure*]. The floor is now open for . . . dis—— [*The* WOMAN IN AVIATRIX'S OUTFIT *has raised her hand.*] Miss . . . Earhart?

Woman in Aviatrix's Outfit. How do you know they're going to attack?

Woman with Gavel. This is a matter of survival, Miss Earhart! Not a matter for *jest!*

Woman in Aviatrix's Outfit. Then tell me how you know the Men's Ward is going to attack.

Woman with Gavel. Miss White's report just *explained* it to you!

Woman in Aviatrix's Outfit. I couldn't follow its logic.

Girl in Gossamer Dress. What!

Woman with Gavel. Are you trying to imply, Miss Earhart, that our lives are *not* in danger?

Commotion! The WOMAN WITH GAVEL *raps her gavel for silence.*

Woman in Aviatrix's Outfit. I am only implying, Miss Anthony, that if they *are* in danger, then perhaps it's due to someone, or someplace, else.

Woman with Gavel. Such as *what?*

Woman in Aviatrix's Outfit [*calmly*]. Such as——

Woman in Safari Outfit. She's just wasting time! *Don't listen to her!*

Woman with Notebook. R-r-r-right!

Silence.

Woman with Gavel. The meeting . . . will now continue. If there are any *oth*—— Miss Earhart, would you mind very much not grinning at me like that?

Woman in Aviatrix's Outfit. So no one's going to answer my question, hm?

Woman with Gavel. Will someone please answer Miss Earhart's idiotic question: "How do we know the Men's Ward is going to attack?"

Woman in Safari Outfit. We simply know, *that's* how!

Girl in Gossamer Dress. Right. We simply *know!*

Woman Who Plays Records. Ve simply *know.*

Woman with Notebook. We s-s-simmmmply know. . . .

Woman with Gavel [smiling in triumph]. Well. I trust *that* answers your question.

Woman in Aviatrix's Outfit [smiling back]. Oh, yes. Yes, thank you. Indeed it does.

The WOMAN IN ARMOR *rises as if in some mesmeric state.*

Woman in Armor [distantly]. Besides. My voices have been telling me for quite some time now, they've been telling me: Joan, fix your pants; they're getting too rusty. And they've been telling me: Joan. Any day now it will all be over. *The attack will come. [And then she sits, slowly.]*

Pause.

Woman with Gavel. All right, ladies. What are we going to do?

Woman in Safari Outfit. Attack *first*, I say! *[Stunned reaction from all.]* Strike while the kettle's boiling, as the cannibals used to put it! Get 'em while the going's good!

Woman Who Plays Records. But—but vould dat *look* right?

Woman in Safari Outfit. It'll look a damn sight better, honey, than waiting on our asses till *they* attack *us!*

Woman Who Plays Records [flustered]. Vell—vell I mean, I mean——

Woman with Gavel. She means—forgive me, dear—she means, I think, that if we attacked the Men's Ward first —unprovoked, so to speak—wouldn't we lose a lot of privileges as a result?

Woman Who Plays Records. Exactly! Like bowling, for instance, vich is something dat means a great deal to me. Laugh if you like.

Woman in Armor. And our annual Christmas party!

We'd lose *that,* I bet. And I *love* that party. I love Christmas.

Girl in Gossamer Dress. And what about our movies twice a month? I bet we wouldn't see *any.*

Woman in Aviatrix's Outfit. Just incredible.

Woman with Notebook. We'd lose a *lot* of th-th-th-things that w-way, I'm af-f-f-fraid.

Woman with Gavel [*turning to the* WOMAN IN SAFARI OUTFIT]. Yes, Mrs. Johnson. I'm afraid we would.

Woman in Safari Outfit [*rising*]. And *I'm* afraid you do me an injustice. I've got no intention of attacking uprovoked.

Woman with Gavel. You *don't?*

Girl in Gossamer Dress. But——

Woman Who Plays Records. Vell how——

Woman in Safari Outfit. You see, I've spent my whole life among wild animals, and when you do that, honey, after a while you get to love 'em. And when you do *that,* honey, you don't like to kill 'em unprovoked. You don't like to kill 'em, shall we say, "just for the fun of it." You don't like to kill 'em for the *trophy.* . . . No. Mother Necessity *alone* pulls the trigger on your gold-plated elephant gun. When you kill, you kill for either of two reasons. You kill 'cause you're being attacked (by tigers, let us say). Or you kill 'cause you're very hungry. Well. You get the point. *Now.* I say we ain't strong enough to wait till the Men's Ward attacks us. Unless, of course, you feel like dying in the process. Which means *we're* the ones who've gotta do the attacking. *But!* I *also* say: it's no good to attack without sufficient provocation.

Girl in Gossamer Dress. Which could mean we'd lose a lot of privileges, right?

Woman in Safari Outfit. Right. Therefore . . . what we need . . . is sufficient *provocation.* [*Applause from the ladies. The* WOMAN WITH GAVEL *raps for silence.*] And here's how we get it. We get it through hunger and thirst, the second of the two justifiable reasons for killing which I've found. And this is the gist of the plan. For the next three days we will refuse all food and drink offered. Then, on the fourth, we will, with God on our side, invade the Men's Ward. And eat them. Then, afterwards, drink their blood.

Woman with Gavel. The proposal is now open for discussion.

Woman in Aviatrix's Outfit. Um, a question. Do I assume correctly when I interpret Mrs. Johnson's proposal as implying, or better yet, presupposing that we——oh, how shall I say it?—*kill* the men first?

Woman in Safari Outfit. Madame President!

Woman with Gavel. The chair, in an effort to maintain parliamentary order, will assume that Miss Earhart's question was raised in good faith. In which case it interprets Mrs. Johnson's proposal—and stop me, please, Mrs. Johnson, if for some reason, I'm wrong—it interprets Mrs. Johnson's proposal as suggesting that we, yes, kill them first.

Woman with Notebook [*sotto voce*]. It would be it would be very difficult, wouldn't it, it would be very difficult, wouldn't it, to . . . to to to . . . to . . . to . . . to do it . . . well, the *other* way?

Woman in Safari Outfit. What's your interest in this, honey? Having some "fun"?

Woman with Notebook. Oh, no, no. No question of f-fun involved. J-j-just . . . curiosity. Just a . . . writer's curiosity. That's all.

Woman with Gavel [*rapping with her gavel*]. The proposal is open for discussion! Ladies? Ah. Mrs. Mozart. Yes?

Woman Who Plays Records. Vell. First of all let me say dat I t'ink de most important t'ing about dis plan is dat at least it's a *vorking* plan. It's a place to begin. And God knows, dat's jus' vat ve need. *Nevertheless.* I t'ink dere are some problems inherent. First: it's not, by a long shot, vat I'd call kosher meat. But den, I'm more Reform dan Ort'odox so it's not really all dat bad. Second! . . . Vit so many big men over dere how do you expect little vomen like us to finish dem all? Vat I mean is, vat vould ve do vit de extras?

Woman in Aviatrix's Outfit. Why wrap them up, of course, and eat them later.

Woman in Safari Outfit. Madame President!

Woman with Gavel [*rapping furiously*]. May I remind you, Miss Earhart, that there's not much time left! And that we can't afford to waste that time on your little jokes.

Woman in Safari Outfit [*sadly, almost to herself*]. She does have a point though, I'm afraid.

Woman in Aviatrix's Outfit. Ah!

Woman in Safari Outfit. Not *you*, you fool!

Woman with Notebook.

Amelia Earhart
Is a dear-heart.

Woman in Safari Outfit. Mrs. Mozart, believe it or not, is the one who has the point.

Woman Who Plays Records. Hah! I t'ought I did. [*The other women pat her on the back and flash smiles of congratulations.*] Vell? Don' keep us in de dark, for heaven's sake. Vat is it?

Woman in Safari Outfit [*finding it hard to speak, defeated*]. The point . . . is this. As it's quite true that we'd never be able to eat them all, yet . . . would obviously have to kill them all, those dead but left uneaten would appear, I'm afraid, to have been killed for the *fun* of it, not the necessity. In other words . . . the uneaten would become our trophies. We'd . . . lose our privileges after all. Madame President . . . ladies . . . my plan is no good.

Everyone stares glumly at the WOMAN IN SAFARI OUTFIT.

Woman in Aviatrix's Outfit [*brightly*]. Well, I say if you can't have a moosehead on the wall, a good man'll do just fine.

But no one pays attention. So, with a shrug, she rests her chin in her hands, bored with it all.

Woman with Gavel. Well . . . any other ideas? [*Silence.*] Girls? . . . I don't think I need remind you that the matter is urgent. [*Silence. Very weakly.*] Girls? . . . Our *lives* are at stake.

Woman in Aviatrix's Outfit [*to herself*]. Yes. Just incredible. The whole thing . . .

But silence has filled the room. The women are lost somewhere in their own private thoughts. It is now that the WOMAN IN QUEENLY SPANISH GARB *rises. She removes her veil. For some reason no one seems to notice. During her entire speech it will be as if, to the others, she is not speaking at all. And when she sits, as if no time has passed.*

Woman in Queenly Spanish Garb. What to do about Columbus—that is what concerns us most. Ferdinand is a bitch, we don't need Aragon. Columbus is the thing. What to do about Columbus. *That* is the thing. . . . Oh, not that he'll reach India, for India lies east not west, as every schoolchild knows. But a new world may well lie west and if it does you can bet that fat idiot will find it! Never sailed before in his life, you know. No knowledge at all of navigation. In fact, terrified of the sea. Well. That's the sort that's dangerous. "Land, ho!" we can hear him cry, his boat run aground in the night (and most likely on some lovely, palm-sheltered beach). *"Land, ho . . ."* "Um, Captain," says his first mate softly, "I think we'd best repair our ship." In the morning, Columbus descends to see just what it is he's run into, finds four hundred bare-breasted maidens drinking coconut milk, and cries, "Curse my luck! *This* isn't India!" . . . Yes. Curse his luck. A new world found. A new world for us to deal with. And, oh, my God, here we are, Queen of Spain, and not yet figured out what to do with this one. [*And then, slowly, she sits.*]

Short pause.

Woman with Gavel. Well. I knew we'd find a way.

Girl in Gossamer Dress. You mean——

Woman with Gavel. I have a plan. Yes.

Woman Who Plays Records. Ve're gonna *live!* [*She starts to cry.*]

Woman with Gavel. If we are, however, then mark *this*.

Our living will depend on swiftness of action and commitment to the cause. It will depend on strength. On silence. And on sacrifice . . . Our living—will depend on *you!*

Woman Who Plays Records. Uh-oh.

Woman with Gavel. Ah, ladies, ladies. I know. I know. How sad it is that times such as these do not lend themselves to lesser problems. And the problems—to easier solutions. [*She smiles sadly.*] It is a difficult era, this one in which we live.

The WOMAN WHO PLAYS RECORDS *starts to cry again.*

Woman in Aviatrix's Outfit. I trust the secretary got that down.

The WOMAN WITH NOTEBOOK *jumps up from her seat and runs over to the aviatrix. She shows her the minutes.*

Woman with Notebook. "The meeting was called to order at the——"

The WOMAN WITH GAVEL *raps her gavel.*

Woman in Aviatrix's Outfit [*to the secretary, sotto voce*]. Ssh. Time for the plan. Better go back and get it down, too. Mustn't have the minutes incomplete. [*The secretary nods and rushes back to her seat. To the* WOMAN WITH GAVEL.] All set, honey. Fire away!

Woman in Armor [*distantly*]. No, don't like the French. They let me down, they did. . . .

Pause. The WOMAN WITH GAVEL *glares at the aviatrix, a cold smile spreading over her face.*

Woman with Gavel. Well. Here is the plan.

Woman Who Plays Records [*to the aviatrix, sotto voce*]. And you be a nice girl, Amelia. Dis is a matter of life and death.

Woman with Gavel. Since, as you all know, we cannot afford to attack the Men's Ward first—yet, at the same time (and for obvious reasons) cannot afford to wait till they attack us—the only thing to do, clearly, is make sure there is *no* attack. By *anyone!* In other words, to insure our safety, ladies, we must make the men believe that we are stronger than we really are.

Short, confused pause.

Woman in Safari Outfit. You mean . . . *bluff* 'em.

Woman with Gavel. Well, I prefer to think of it more as *frighten* them. If you see what I mean.

Woman in Aviatrix's Outfit. Oh, clear as day.

Woman with Gavel. Ah, Miss Earhart. If only you could know how thrilling it is to me, as president of this committee, to know that there is, amongst us, one as perceptive as *you*. For the benefit of those others, however, not quite as fortunate—and I must, in all honesty, say I number myself among *these*—I will now take the time to explain more—try to make my plan a little clearer. Amelia, my dear, *please try and bear with us.* [*She smiles at the* WOMAN IN AVIATRIX's OUTFIT. *The others glare at her angrily.*] Ladies, what we must do is kill someone.

Woman in Aviatrix's Outfit. Huh?

Stunned silence.

Woman Who Plays Records. Vat?

Woman with Notebook. K-k-kill-l-l someone?

Woman with Gavel. Yes. Kill someone. Anyone at all.

Woman in Safari Outfit. But . . . I thought we decided——

Woman Who Plays Records. Right! I t'ought ve decided——

Woman in Safari Outfit. Oh, shut up!

Girl in Gossamer Dress. Yes. Didn't we——

Woman with Gavel. Ladies! [*They quiet down. With a laugh.*] I don't mean kill one of *them*. I mean——

Woman Who Plays Records. Oi gevalt!

Woman in Aviatrix's Outfit. What the——

Woman in Safari Outfit. Look, I don't——

Girl in Gossamer Dress. Bu——

Woman with Gavel. Ladies!

Woman in Armor. My pants are getting rusty!

Woman with Gavel. Ladies!

Woman with Notebook [*her head buried in her notebook*]. "The m-meeting was c-called to——"

Woman with Gavel. Ladies, please! ! [*She raps them*

quiet.] Be patient for a minute, *please*. Now. Just think of this: a body—for argument's sake, *mine*, let us say sent in the dead of night, arriving at the Men's Ward first thing in the morning, our signatures attached. Well! I ask you, would *that* be a warning or wouldn't it? Would *that* frighten the Men's Ward or wouldn't it? Would *that* be a show of strength, a show of power, of intention? Or wouldn't it!

Stunned reaction from all except the aviatrix.

Woman in Aviatrix's Outfit. Actually, with all those signatures, it *might* be rather impressive at that.

Girl in Gossamer Dress. Amelia, for God's sakes, this is no time to joke around.

Woman with Gavel. Furthermore! If that didn't work, we could send another one in the afternoon, then perhaps another the following morning. Oh, yes, they'd soon get the point. They'd soon realize that *they could be next.* . . . Well. Who shall it be?

Woman in Aviatrix's Outfit. I thought I heard you suggest *yourself.*

Woman with Gavel. That was just an example. *Ladies?*

Short pause before the furor breaks loose.

Woman in Safari Outfit. Joan of Arc's the one!

The WOMAN IN ARMOR *leaps up.*

Woman with Notebook. Yes! I s-s-second the——

Woman in Armor [*advancing on the secretary, her crucifix raised like a tomahawk*].
Gertrude Stein
Will now be mine.

Woman with Notebook. I ch-change my vote to-to *Pearl White!*

Girl in Gossamer Dress. What!

Woman in Armor. That's better.

Girl in Gossamer Dress. Mrs. Mozart! Look at *her!* She'd be better yet!

Woman Who Plays Records. Vat?

Woman in Safari Outfit. Yeah. Teach her to make that goddamn racket!

Woman Who Plays Records. Racket? Vat means by a——

Woman with Notebook [*advancing, pencil poised like a knife*]. Ha-hahhh.

Woman Who Plays Records. Look! Now look! I t'ink maybe you should consider, um . . .

Woman in Armor. Osa Johnson! Let's kill Osa Johnson! Let's all kill Osa Johnson!

Woman Who Plays Records. My choice exactly!

Woman in Safari Outfit [*wielding her toy gun like a club*]. You come near me and I'll——

Girl in Gossamer Dress. Kill Osa Johnson! Let's all kill Osa Johnson!

Woman in Safari Outfit [*advancing on the* GIRL IN GOSSAMER DRESS]. I'm gonna wring your little blonde neck once and for all!

Girl in Gossamer Dress. Gertrude Stein! I've changed my vote to Gertrude Stein!

Woman in Armor. Yes! Gertrude Stein!

Girl in Gossamer Dress. Not Osa Johnson! Gertrude——

Woman with Notebook. Mrs.——

Woman with Notebook	To-	Mozart!
Girl in Gossamer Dress	gether	Pearl——
Woman Who Plays Records		White! Pearl White!
	To-	
Girl in Gossamer Dress	gether	Gertrude Stein!
Woman with Notebook		Joan of Arc!
Woman Who Plays Records		Pearl White! Pearl White!
Girl in Gossamer Dress		Gertrude Stein! Gertrude Stein!
Woman with Notebook	To-	J-Joan of Arc! J-Joan of Arc!
Woman in Safari Outfit	gether	Mrs. Mozart! Mrs. Mozart!
Woman in Armor		Osa Johnson! Osa Johnson!

Woman Who Plays Records		Osa Johnson! Osa Johnson!
Girl in Gossamer Dress		Mrs. Mozart! Mrs. Mozart!
Woman with Notebook	*To-* *gether*	P-Pearl White! P-Pearl White!
Woman in Safari Outfit		Joan of Arc! Joan of Arc!
Woman in Armor		Gertrude Stein! Gertrude Stein!

Woman in Aviatrix's Outfit. You mean no one's going to mention poor Isabella?

They turn en masse to the WOMAN IN QUEENLY SPANISH GARB.

All. Isabella. *Isabella!*

The WOMAN IN QUEENLY SPANISH GARB *rises in terror.*

Woman in Aviatrix's Outfit. Hah! So she *does* hear.

All. So she does hear! !

Woman with Gavel. Ladies! Ladies! [*They all look back just as they're about to strike down the* WOMAN IN QUEENLY SPANISH GARB.] *My vote*—for what it's worth— goes to *Miss Earhart.* . . . [*To the* WOMAN IN AVIATRIX'S OUTFIT.] Nothing personal, darling. You understand.

They all turn and start toward the aviatrix.

Woman in Aviatrix's Outfit. Now wait a minute. Wait a minute! . . . Now look. Hold on. *Hold on!*

Woman with Gavel. Dear, please try and understand. It's for the Cause. It's for our lives. Self-sacrifice, you see, is the only way. . . . So help us just this once. *Will you?*

They surround her and back her into the arc of the table.

Woman in Aviatrix's Outfit. Now look. Now look! Now *wait a second!*

Girl in Gossamer Dress. Please, Amelia. Try and understand.

Woman Who Plays Records. It's hard, I know. But, believe me, it's de only vay. And you know I vouldn't tell no lie.

Woman in Aviatrix's Outfit. Look, wait a second! *Look, fun's fun but this—— [She is backed into the arc, no escape. The* WOMAN IN SAFARI OUTFIT *spots the unguarded crucifix of the* WOMAN IN ARMOR. *While everyone is advancing on the aviatrix, she cracks the crucifix in two.]* I said wait, will you! *Wait . . . ! [As they are about to strangle her.]* But I am Amelia Earhart. I tell you I really am . . .

And then they start to strangle her. The WOMAN IN SAFARI OUTFIT *rushes into the circle, the wooden crossbar of the crucifix brandished high like a club.*

Woman in Safari Outfit. Lemme at her! Lemme at her!

When the circle splits to let the WOMAN IN SAFARI OUTFIT *through, the* WOMAN IN AVIATRIX'S OUTFIT, *not yet dead but almost, manages to break out.*

Woman in Armor [seeing her broken crucifix]. Aghhhh! *[She grabs the piece of wood from the* WOMAN IN SAFARI OUTFIT'S *hands. The* WOMAN IN AVIATRIX'S OUTFIT, *too stunned to run, merely backs away.]* It came with the armor! It *came with the armor! [When the* WOMAN IN AVIATRIX'S OUTFIT *finally decides to run, she is caught and dragged back into the circle. The* WOMAN IN ARMOR *picks up her broken pieces of wood and, clutching them to her breast, goes off to a corner of the room, sobbing.]* It came with the armor. It *came with the armor. . . .*

Woman in Safari Outfit. Agh! Lemme at her! I'll show you how it's done!

Whereupon the circle of women proceeds to strangle the WOMAN IN AVIATRIX'S OUTFIT *to death. The ones on the periphery bang on the table, on the floor, on anything they can find, in tribal beat. Of these women, the* WOMAN WITH NOTEBOOK *has climbed up on the table itself and is looking down, recording the event. The* GIRL IN GOSSAMER DRESS *suddenly rushes out of the circle with the aviatrix's parachute and goggles.*

Girl in Gossamer Dress. I've got her goggles! I've got her goggles! I've got her silken sheet! *[She starts to dance*

about, the goggles being used as a brassiere, the silk para-
chute as a vamp's dress.]

> I'm Theda Bara,
> Not Pearl White!
> And those who disagree
> Just aren't *right!*

The WOMAN WITH NOTEBOOK *starts to rip up her note-*
book paper and drop it, like snow, over the scene of the
crime.

Woman with Notebook. The snow! The snow! Look
at the snow! Look at the snow! Look at it falling! Falling.
Falling. Look at the snow! Look at the snow! Look at it
falling! Falling. Falling!

About now the WOMAN IN QUEENLY SPANISH GARB *no-*
tices the GIRL IN GOSSAMER DRESS *dancing and starts to*
dance a flamenco. Unfortunately, she does not dance very
well.

Woman in Safari Outfit [*breaking from the circle and*
pacing about]. Where's the pot? Where's the goddamned
pot? How the hell can we send her over there if we
haven't cooked her in the pot?

Gradually the women are losing interest in the mangled
and long-dead body of the aviatrix. And so they start to
drift away, to leave the scene of the crime as if nothing
had happened at all.

Woman with Notebook [*the last one at the scene of*
the crime]. Look at the snow. Look at the snow. Look
at it falling, falling, falling. . . .

Woman in Armor [*to the* WOMAN IN SAFARI OUTFIT,
like a child]. Why did you do that? Why did you have
to do that? It was mine. It came with the armor. It was
mine. You had no right to do that. Why did you have to
do that?

The WOMAN IN ARMOR *cluches the pieces of wood to*
her breast and sits, sobbing very softly. The WOMAN IN
SAFARI OUTFIT *turns away.*

Woman in Safari Outfit [*to the* WOMAN WITH GAVEL]. You haven't seen a pot around, have you? A small, black pot. Just big enough for one? [*She doesn't wait for an answer but shuffles off, looking.*]

Woman with Gavel. Yes. I knew we'd find a way. A plan. A way.

Girl in Gossamer Dress [*wrapping herself up like a cocoon*]. It's so soft. So soft. I knew it would be this soft.

Woman with Gavel. So we'll send it over in the morning, signatures attached. First, though, I must get my gavel fixed. Needs a little fixing. Seems a little weak.

Girl in Gossamer Dress. I've always wanted something just this soft. And something to put over my chest.

The women start gradually to reassemble. The lights have faded a bit. The WOMAN WHO PLAYS RECORDS *is sitting at the table, staring at the broken record in her hands. Suddenly, from far away, the Andante from Mozart's Quartet in F Major is heard. No one hears. The women are slowly winding down, like spring toys overplayed. The* WOMAN IN QUEENLY SPANISH GARB *stops spinning about. The* WOMAN IN SAFARI OUTFIT *walks more slowly in her search. The* WOMAN IN ARMOR *rocks back and forth less. The* WOMAN WITH NOTEBOOK *drops snowflakes elsewhere, the body forgotten. She moves slowly as she goes. The* GIRL IN GOSSAMER DRESS *wraps herself up at the table—but in a different seat. The* WOMAN WITH GAVEL *is examining her gavel. And then the* WOMAN WHO PLAYS RECORDS *hears! No one else is able to. She jumps up, rushes to the window, and opens it. She stares up at the sky.*

Woman Who Plays Records. Volfgang! Ah! My little Volfgang! I hear you calling! I hear you calling. Vat is it, my love? [*She listens as the Mozart plays on. The women are slowly starting to sit at the table, though they do not take the same places as before.*] Yes, yes, my love. Of course I see your point. But you must try and understand ours. Volfgang! *Please,* my lover. You made my poor life so happy. Don't be angry vit me now.

*The women, having seated themselves, look about the
table and realize that something is wrong.*

Girl in Gossamer Dress [*softly*]. It's Amelia.

Woman with Notebook. Yes. A-m-m-melia.

Woman with Gavel. Amelia is the one who's missing.

They look about their chairs, puzzled.

Woman Who Plays Records. Volfgang! Ssh, Volfgang.
Listen for a minute. *Listen for a minute.* Vill you ever
forget the day you began *Don Giovanni?*

Woman with Gavel [*leaning over the table and spotting the aviatrix on the floor*]. There she is.

They all lean over and stare at the limp body. The
WOMAN WITH GAVEL *whispers to the woman beside her,
who in turn whispers to the woman beside her. They rise
and drag the aviatrix back to the table. They prop her
up in her old chair. Naturally she flops across the table.
The women, shrugging, go back and sit down. All of this
occurs during the* WOMAN WHO PLAYS RECORDS' *last
speech.*

Woman Who Plays Records. Ahhhh, I remember. I
remember I touched your hand dat morning. But for
some reason I didn't know it den. But den. *Den* ven you
looked at me vit dos eyes of yours. And ven I saw vit
mine own two eyes dos eyes of yours, *den!* Yes. *Den I
knew.* . . . And I said to myself, Ah, my little Volfgang,
mein liebchen Volfgang, today you vill begin *Don Giovanni.*

And the WOMAN WHO PLAYS RECORDS *stares out the
window, the music still there. And then suddenly, the*
WOMAN WITH GAVEL *sits up tall. She stares at the door.
The other women follow suit.*

Woman with Notebook. Pssst.

The WOMAN WHO PLAYS RECORDS *turns. She under-
stands. She rushes back to her seat. The door opens and
the* ASSISTANT *enters the room. He walks behind the
women. He stops behind the slumped figure of the aviatrix.*

Assistant. Sleeping, hm? . . . Ah well, can't say I blame you. It's been a long day—*curious* day. Yes. Curious day this has been. . . . [*Distantly, really to himself.*] From the moment I got up, something in the air. Like the women outside, for instance, lined up in their rocking chairs and laughing away. Well, they've done that before, of course. But yet . . . *just laughing away* . . . What is it they claim now? Oh, yes. That the sun has gone forever and now there will be only night. "Look at the moon!" they say. "There isn't any, tonight," I say. And then they grin. . . . Then! Yes, then they say, in those strange voices of theirs, "Go and check and you will find the clocks have broken." Well. That can all be explained, of course. Someone at the clocks, no doubt. (Though God only knows why.) Yet, the curious way they say, "We don't *need* the clocks any more." The way they say they know the hour anyhow. And then laugh. And . . . rock back and forth in those chairs. Though—yes, their *eyes* really are the thing. The lights were down. A bulb I guess had broken. And some-how their eyes, like cats' eyes, seemed to be glowing in the dark. [*He stares at the window for a few moments. Then realizes that it's open. He goes over to it.*] Ladies. You must keep the windows closed. [*He closes it. The Mozart disappears.*] Must keep the windows closed.

And then, while the ASSISTANT *stands there and the women sit motionless behind him, one woman slumped at the table, the lights fade.*

Curtain.

THE QUESTIONING OF NICK

A Play in One Act

CHARACTERS

Nick Carmonatti
Sergeant Prunchink
Lieutenant Carling

Scene—The office of Police Lieutenant Carling

THE QUESTIONING OF NICK

It is the office of LIEUTENANT CARLING: *cold and drab, a "typical" room for the lieutenant of a small suburban county police force.*

Sitting on the edge of the only desk in the room is SERGEANT PRUNCHINK. *He is busy glancing through a folder and trying his hardest to pay no attention to* NICK CARMONATTI, *the other person in the room.* NICK *is standing at a window in the rear of the room, staring out. He wears dungarees and a soiled T-shirt.*

Having tired of the view, NICK *turns from the window and stalks about, trying his hardest to annoy the sergeant. He yawns, belches, and finally clears his nose with a sound comparable to that of a clogged-up vacuum cleaner.* SERGEANT PRUNCHINK *pays no attention. The door opens.* LIEUTENANT CARLING *enters. Hearing the door,* NICK *turns and goes back to the window. He stares out.* LIEUTENANT CARLING *walks directly to a large filing cabinet without seeming to notice* NICK. *He opens a drawer, leafs through a section of it, and finds the folder he wants.*

CARLING. So here we are: "Mr. Nicholas Vincento Carmonatti." I didn't think it would be too long. It wasn't too long. Was it, Nick?

Prunchink. Some guys just aren't smart.

NICK *turns from the window, stares at* PRUNCHINK, *walks over, and spits at his feet.* PRUNCHINK *rises, fists clenched.*

CARLING. Let him alone, Stan. [PRUNCHINK *sits.*] This time he's had it.

Nick. You guys make me laugh.

Carling. Where were you last night, Nick?

NICK *laughs and turns away from them.*

Prunchink. Last night, Nick. At ten thirty. Where were you? [*Silence.*] Nick! I'm asking you a question!

Nick. Wouldn't ya like to know. Go on, ask yer wife. *She'll* tell ya. [NICK *winks at* PRUNCHINK.]

Carling. Nick, we'd like you to tell us what you did last night.

Prunchink. You might just as well, Nick. Stanikowski's told us everything.

Carling. They took him to St. Francis this morning. Fractured skull and five broken ribs. He says you're the man.

Nick. I never touched the guy. I was home all night.

Carling. It could go bad with you if you weren't telling the truth, Nick.

Nick. How come you guys are makin' such a big fuss over a fight? I've had ten broken ribs an' no one ever did nothin'.

Carling. Just tell us what happened, Nick. That's all we want to know.

Nick. I tol' ya, I was home.

Prunchink. All night?

Nick. Yeah. All night.

Prunchink. Then how come Stanikowski said it was you?

Nick. He was wrong! Maybe he was thinkin' of my brother. He's *always* beatin' guys up.

Carling. All right, Nick. You know why you're here. If you're gonna tell us what happened, go ahead. But don't waste our time if you're not gonna talk. We'll just hold you on an open charge till you do.

Nick. Who's sayin' I don' wanna talk? I'll talk, I'll talk. [*Pause.*] I was home. [CARLING *sighs and heads for the door.* NICK *takes a step, as if to stop him from leaving.*] It was jus' an ordinary fight. [CARLING *stops. He turns back and faces* NICK.] You know, guys get a little pissed off, so . . . they fight. That's all. Nothin' to get so goddam excited about. [*Long pause.*] It must've been somewhere about eleven or twelve. I remember comin' outa MacFarlen's and wond'rin' where to go, 'cause I was hungry. (Funny how ya always get hungry 'bout then.) Well, I look across the street an' I see the Giraffe standin' there, puttin' the make on these two chicks, see. I remember they——

Prunchink. Who's the Giraffe?

Nick. Stanikowski. That's who ya wanna hear about, ain't it? [PRUNCHINK *nods.*] Well, like I said before I was interrupted, there he was puttin' the make on these two chicks. Well. Since there was two of 'em I figure he wouldn't mind so I walk over like I ain't seen 'im in ten years an', pretty soon, start talkin' to one of these two chicks. Well . . . that was it. The Giraffe wasn't too happy to see me, I guess he wanted 'em for himself, so when they left he started yellin' an' . . . we had a fight. That's all.

Prunchink. Oh, that's all.

Carling. Well, I guess Stanikowski was wrong then. 'Cause if Nick says that's all——

Nick. That's all! Just a fight. I didn't mean to beat 'im up as bad as I did, but that's all. I swear.

NICK *turns defiantly and goes to the window.* CARLING *walks over to* PRUNCHINK *and whispers something in his ear.* PRUNCHINK *nods.* CARLING *goes back and sits on the edge of the desk. He glances through* NICK's *folder for a few moments. When he first talks he does not look up, so the question comes as a surprise.*

Carling. Suppose you tell us about your basketball team.

Nick. . . . What?

Carling. Your basketball team. You have a basketball team at school, don't you? [NICK *nods weakly.*] Well. Suppose you tell us about it.

Nick. I don' get it. Wha' d'ya wanna know? [CARLING *leans back, stares at* NICK *for a few moments, then shrugs.*] I mean, ya wanna know who plays, or when we practice, or what?

Carling. Anything at all, Nick. Why you like to play, how many points you've scored. Anything at all.

Nick. I don' get it.

Carling. Get what?

Nick. Why you guys are so interested in the team.

Carling. Well, I'll tell you, Nick. Since your fight with Stanikowski's been settled, we've got a whole afternoon to kill. We hear you're a good ballplayer, that's all.

Prunchink. We've seen your picture in the paper, Nick. You must be a *big man*.

Nick [*nonchalantly*]. Well . . . I donno what to tell

you guys. I'm the center on the team. There's, uh, Venezio
an' Watkins at forward, an' Stanikowski an' Trapoti at
guard. We got a——

Prunchink. Who's gonna play guard now?

Nick. Huh?

Prunchink. Now that Stanikowski's out. Who's gonna
take his place?

Nick. Oh . . . Meltener or Malone. I donno who.
Maybe even Porkavitch. We got a——

Carling. Stanikowski was pretty good, wasn't he?

Nick. Who? The *Giraffe?* Egh. Sometimes. Sometimes
no. You know what I mean. He wasn't . . . *dependable.*

Carling and *Prunchink.* Oh.

Nick. We got a twelve an' two record an' we're in second place. Last year the team——

Carling. Didn't you just lose to Rockville the other
day?

Nick. Yeah. Last year the team——

Carling. I heard that was a pretty close game.

Prunchink. Lost in the last few minutes, didn't you?
Blew a *big lead?*

Nick [*clapping his hands in applause*]. Hey, that's right.
That's right. Really good. Real smar-r-rt. Ya read the
papers, I see. Listen, you guys wan' me to tell you about
the team, or ya wanna turn this into a quiz show? Now
wha' d'ya say?

Carling. I'm sorry, Nick. We were just curious.

Nick. Chrissake. All you guys are the same.

Carling. We just wondered how you felt missing that
shot?

Nick. I felt bad.

Carling. No hard feelings, Nick?

Nick. Nah, no hard feelings. Ya wan' me to tell ya about
the team?

Carling. Go ahead, Nick.

Nick. Well. Last year an' the year before we won the
championship, an' I was named in *Sport* as one of the five
hun'red leading basketball prospects in the whole country.

Prunchink. That's very good, Nick.

Nick. That year I scored, lemme see, two hun'red an'——

Carling. I'm sorry, Nick. Would you excuse me for a moment?

Nick [*irritated*]. Go ahead.

Carling. Stan, where's that report on Ferranchi?

NICK *starts at the name of Ferranchi, but* CARLING *and* PRUNCHINK *do not seem to notice.*

Prunchink. I thought I put it under the Jefferson case.

Carling [*leafing through papers and finding it*]. Yeah. I've got it. Here it is. [*He glances through it; then puts it down.*] I'm sorry, Nick. What were you saying?

Nick. Let's see, uh . . . we got a twelve an' two record and, uh, I've scored——

Prunchink. You said that already, Nick.

Nick. Oh. Did I?

Prunchink. Hm-hm.

Nick. Oh . . . Well, with you guys always interruptin' me it's no wonder I can't think.

Prunchink. We understand, Nick.

Nick. What else you wanna know?

Carling [*looking up from the Ferranchi report*]. Oh, I'm sorry, Nick, but I didn't hear what you said.

Nick. Lookit. I've told you guys all there is to know about the team. My ol' lady cleans the tables over at Strakey's an' I gotta sweep up the front walk. Wha' d'ya say, can I go?

NICK *starts toward the door.* PRUNCHINK *blocks his way.*

Prunchink. What's your hurry, Nick? You can get that done later.

Nick. Yeah. But——

Prunchink. You've got a whole afternoon. There's no rush.

NICK *shrugs, turns, and walks back to the window sill.*

Carling. Nick, who's your captain?

Nick. Huh?

Carling. Who's the captain of your team?

Nick. Oh, the captain, uh . . . I'm not sure. Ya see,

he never does much. Um, I think it was Watkins. But I'm not sure. [NICK *notices the reaction on* PRUNCHINK'*s face to this statement.*] No, no, it was, it was the Giraffe, I think. I'm not sure.

Carling. He must've been a good player then, huh?

Nick. Who? Giraffe? I told ya already. *He wasn't dependable.*

Prunchink. But I always thought the *best* guy was made captain.

Nick. Nah!

Carling. That's what I've always heard.

Nick. Nah. Not our team. Maybe some others, but, no, not ours. I mean, I don' wanna say this, but it's usually the coach's guy. You know . . .

Prunchink. Yeah. I know. Who *was* the best guy, Nick?

Nick. Well-l-l-l, it's hard for me to say.

Carling. I heard Watkins was really good.

Nick. I donno. He don' dribble too good. He's always palmin' the ball. You know, real "Fancy Dan." Goes this way, goes that way, an' he loses the ball, so where are ya? He ain't good for the team.

Carling. Tomkins of the *News* said Watkins was great.

Nick. When'd he say that?

Carling. I don't remember. I think it was last week.

Nick. You ever seen 'im play? [CARLING *shakes his head.*] He ain't so hot.

Carling. Tomkins even thinks he might win the Rosewell Award.

Nick. Him? Agh, that guy donno what he's talkin' about. There lots of guys better. .

Prunchink. Even the *Herald* likes him, Nick. Joe Stanley's column picked him as one of the best college prospects around.

Nick [*to* PRUNCHINK]. What, you too? Look, the papers get it from the coach. You don' think those guys 'ud take the time to see one of *our* games, do ya? I'm tellin' ya, the coach likes guys sort of . . . you know. Ya can't listen to 'em, that's all. I'm *tellin' ya!*

Carling. Well, if it isn't him, who could it be?

Nick. Well-l-l-l, like I said, it's a hard thing for *me* to say. I mean I'm the——

Prunchink. You're not helping us much, Nick.

Carling. Put it this way, suppose you were a guy who had a lot of dough bet on one of your games, and you wanted to protect your bet by paying off some of the players, which ones would you pay?

Nick. Hm?

Carling. Who would you pay off if you wanted to fix a game?

Nick. Well. That depends on the team.

Carling. Take your team, Nick.

Nick. That's a screwy question to ask. How the hell should *I* know?

Carling. We were just curious.

Nick. Well, I donno.

Prunchink. We figured the guy they'd pay 'ud be the best guy on the team.

Nick. Oh, no, no. That don' necessar'ly figure.

Carling. Oh? How come?

Nick. Well, I mean, it depends on the game. Like, take Watkins for instance. He's a good passer. A game ya need a good passer ya might pay him. See?

Carling. What if it's a game where you need the best *all-around* player?

Nick. Well . . . then . . . I guess . . . I donno. I guess ya'd pay off the best all-around player. [*He laughs.*] Figures, don' it? Seems like a silly question to me.

Prunchink. Why, Nick?

Nick. I donno. I jus' don' see any sense in it, that's all.

Carling. But what if someone were *really* trying to fix your games?

Nick. Hah! *Our* games? Oh, come on, lieutenant, we're *high school*. No one comes to see us.

Carling. Then you haven't been looking up in the stands lately. [Nick *laughs and shrugs his shoulders.*] What about Al Ferranchi?

Nick. Who?

Carling. Al Ferranchi.

Nick. What about 'im?

Carling. We want you to tell us what you know about him.

Nick. Who is he?

CARLING *nods to* PRUNCHINK. PRUNCHINK *takes a pad of paper from his pocket and reads from it.*

Prunchink. "Alfredo Ferranchi; age, thirty-eight; height, five foot eight; weight, approximately one hundred and ninety pounds; bald, brown eyes with large mole over left eye and scar under chin. Married when sixteen. Annulled after one week. Goes by the nickname 'Pojo.' Bowls for MacFarlen's Tavern. No known source of income. Arrested in '38 for armed robbery, sentence two years. Arrested in '43 for counterfeiting ten-dollar bills, sentence ten years, let off after six for good behavior. Suspected for the past two years of pushing dope and booking high-school football and basketball games."

Nick. Jesus. Wha' d'you guys do, sleep with 'im?

Carling. We want you to tell us if you know him.

Nick. I really can't say.

Prunchink. Seen usually around the high school? Never with guys his own age?

Nick. I told ya, I really can't say.

Carling. We think you can, Nick.

Prunchink. He's the one who's always wearing the Mac-Farlen's jacket. You *must* have seen 'im.

Nick [*shrugging at first as if he doesn't know and then snapping his fingers as if suddenly he does*]. O-o-o-oh . . . I think I know the guy ya mean. The one with the pushed-in nose? That funny sort of . . . [PRUNCHINK *nods.*] Yeah, yeah. I think I know the one ya mean.

Carling. How many times have you spoken to him?

Nick. I don' . . . know if I ever have.

Carling. Did he ever talk to you about basketball?

Nick. I'm tellin' ya, lieutenant, I hardly know the guy. I don't think I've spoken to 'im more'n once at the most.

Carling. You sure that's all?

Nick. Yeah, that's all. I'd remember if I did, wouldn't I?

A *pause.* CARLING *sighs and nods at* PRUNCHINK. PRUN-
CHINK *opens the pad of paper again.*

Carling. We spoke to Porkavitch this morning. He said
he'd seen you with Ferranchi a lot lately.

Prunchink. "I've seen them together almost every afternoon after practice."

Nick. Don' listen to that guy. He ain't got no brains.

Prunchink. I thought you two were friends.

Nick. Sure we're friends. But jus' 'cause he's always with
me don' mean he's gotta have brains.

Carling. He told us you needed money because your
mother wasn't making enough for herself, you, and your
brother.

Nick. That's what he said, huh?

Carling. He said you were flashing a roll of bills around
the school after the Rockville loss. Making like a big shot.

Nick. "He said. He said." Hah! He's so goddam stupid
an' so goddam poor that two bucks 'ud look like a roll of
bills to 'im.

Carling. He told us you were running after all the girls.
He told us how the whole school was laughing at you, the
way you were asking them all to go out with you. Nick, it
was embarrassing. He was making *fun* of you.

Nick. He was lyin' through his teeth.

Prunchink. He told us a *lot* of things, Nick.

Nick. He was *lyin'!* Are you guys so stupid ya can't tell
when someone's lyin' to ya? I'm tellin' ya, don' listen to
'im.

Carling. All we're telling you is what Porkavitch told us
this morning.

Nick. But he don' know what he's talkin' about. You
should know some of the things that come outa that guy's
mouth. He donno what he's talkin' about!

Prunchink. Come on, Nick. Why don't you tell us how
much you got?

Carling. If you tell us, it won't go so bad.

Nick [*stunned*]. Tell you what?

Carling. How much you got. That's all we want to
know.

Prunchink. How many times you shaved points, Nick.

Carling. Come on, Nick, tell us!

Prunchink. Tell us, Nick!

Nick. Goddam it! I donno!

A *pause.*

Carling. Don't know what?

Prunchink. What's the matter, Nick? Can't you keep track of all the money?

Nick. Mon—*I didn't say that.* Chris'. You guys twist everything I say. You don'——

Carling. Look, Nick. The truth is, we're not accusing you of anything. We know you're not the one they'd want to pay. Like you said, he'd be the *best* guy on the team. We just figured that by getting you a little angry you might tell us who that was. That's all.

Nick *sits weakly in a chair near the desk.*

Nick. Well, I can't.

Prunchink [*moving his chair a little closer to* Nick's]. Then maybe you can tell us why they kicked you out of the Black Angels.

Nick. What!

Prunchink. We heard the Black Angels didn't want you any more.

Nick. You're crazy.

Prunchink. That's what we heard.

Nick [*rising with clenched fists*]. Who told you that?

Prunchink. That's not important.

Nick [*advancing toward* Prunchink]. I wanna know who told you that!

Prunchink. Were you chicken, Nick? Is that it?

Nick. I wanna know who told you that! It *ain't so!*

Prunchink. Is that it, Nick? Weren't you good enough?

Nick [*grabbing* Prunchink *by the collar*]. *Tell me who told ya! I wanna know who told ya th*—— [Prunchink *shoves* Nick *away.* Nick *staggers back and almost falls.* Carling *and* Prunchink *begin to laugh.* Nick *stands bewildered.*] That ain't the truth. I swear it ain't. The Black

Angels split up. I was with 'em till the end. I swear. *Stop laughing!*

Carling [*with a great grin*]. But Porkavitch said the Black Angels still exist.

Nick. That's what he said, huh? Well, I'm tellin' ya they ain't the same ones.

Carling. He says they are.

Nick. He's crazy.

Carling. Well. He seemed to know what he was talking about.

Nick. Lookit. I'm the guy that got Porkavitch *into* the club. Without me he'd never have been in it. The other guys didn't want 'im. But I said, "Let 'im in." An' *he's* tellin' you it's still the same club?

Carling. That's what he told us.

Nick. Listen. I'll tell ya somethin'. You know what he is in that club? A *nothin'*. That's what he is. He's a *nothin'!*

Prunchink. He told us the guys thought you were a bag of hot air. He said they didn't want *you* in the club.

Nick. That bastard! That shows ya. I take 'im into the club, I tell the guys to be nice to 'im, I get it all set so's they don' pick on 'im all the time, an' look what he goes an' says. I wish to hell he were here right now.

Carling. What would you do, Nick?

Nick. Wha' d'ya mean, what would I do? Ya think someone's gonna get away with sayin' somethin' like that about Nicky Carmonatti? Hah! You got another guess comin'. That guy is nothin' but a punk. A p-u-n-k: punk. He don' *deserve* to be where he is.

Carling. Where *is* he? [NICK *starts. He looks at* CAR-LING *and then at* PRUNCHINK. *There is a blank, frightened look on his face.*] You said, "He doesn't deserve to be where he is." What did you mean by that, Nick?

Nick. I didn't mean nothin'.

Carling. Then why did you say it, Nick?

Nick. I donno. I jus' said it. It didn't mean nothin'. A guy can say things he don' mean.

Prunchink [*to* CARLING]. Maybe he meant that Porka-vitch is the *head* of the Black Angels while he's not even *in* the club.

Nick. No-o-o-o.

Carling. That's what *I* thought he meant. Is that what you meant, Nick?

Nick. No. No! I *told* ya! I didn't mean *nothin'*. What are you guys doin'?

Carling. But Porkavitch *is* the head of the Black Angels, isn't he?

Nick. I told ya there's no club.

Prunchink. You mean there's no club for *you*, Nick.

Nick. There's no club at *all.* Period! Period! There's *no club!*

Carling. Now, why don't you quit kidding us, Nick. We know as well as you do that the Black Angels are still around.

Nick. I told ya, they busted up. Ya can't listen to that Porkavitch. It ain't my fault he's got somethin' against me. We jus' never got along. Ya can't take his word 'cause he's out for me. Don't ya understand? He's *out for me!*

Carling. Nick, you know what Porkavitch told us today?

Nick. I told ya, don' listen to what he says.

Carling. You know what he told us today, Nick? And we were surprised, 'cause we'd always thought you were a big man. Well, you know what he did when we asked him if he thought you'd thrown a game? He laughed. He laughed, Nick. That's what he did. He laughed. "What, pay *him* to throw a game? What for? He misses all the shots anyway." And you know what else he said about you, Nick? He said you're hot air. He said you're big talk, always gonna do things no one else can do. Only you can't do 'em either. You can't fight, or play ball, or do anything. You're a nothing, Nick. A *big, big nothing.* And no one in his right mind would pay you for throwing a game. And then he laughed again, Nick. That's what he did. He just sat back, right where you're sitting now, and laughed. . . . Go on, go home. We don't need you. You just wasted our time. [CARLING *stares at* NICK, *who is fighting to control his tears.*] Look, cry outside, will you? We've got other things to do. [PRUNCHINK *rises from his chair and walks over to* CARLING. *They seem oblivious of* NICK. CARLING *finally looks up.*] Well, are you going or not?

Nick. That's what ya think, huh? . . . I can go home. Ya don' care. All right, *all right!* Let me tell *you* somethin'! [NICK *rises defiantly and points at* PRUNCHINK.] Go get yer pencil, pig face. I'm gonna show ya how stupid you guys are! [NICK *stands with arms akimbo, waiting for* PRUNCHINK *to pick up a pencil.*] Ya ready? All right. I, me, Nicky Carmonatti, me, alone, me, I threw the game. Ya hear that? I was the guy who got paid. No one else. Jus' me. An' I'm the only one that *ever* got paid. . . . Ya wanna know somethin' else, too? I'm the guy who *thought up* the Black Angels! But they never did nothin'. It was the guys in the club. So ya know what I did? I busted 'em up, that's what I did. It ain't any of my troubles that some lousy punks come an' make another club with the same name. Oh, don' worry. They asked me to join. They keep comin' up to me all the time. "Come on, Nick," they say. "Come on. Don' be mad." All the time. An' ya know what I do? I tell 'em, "Eat it!" I wouldn't be seen dead with them guys. A guy's gotta be careful about the guys he's seen with, I say. I'm the only one in this town that got into *Sport Magazine.* I already got an offer from a college. I betcha didn't know that, did ya? No. No. Ya couldn't know that, 'cause *no one* did. I kept it a secret. Let 'em wait, I said. Let 'em wait. They'll see. . . . An' another coach said he was in'erested in me. Yeah! He tol' me himself. An' when *they* tell ya somethin' you *know* that's pretty good. Nah. Let 'em wait, I said. Let 'em wait. They'll see. Hm! I showed those bastards. Hah! I showed 'em. [*The room grows quiet.* CARLING *jots a few things down in a notebook.* PRUNCHINK *walks to the filing cabinet.*] Well, is that enough for you guys? [*Neither* CARLING *nor* PRUNCHINK *seems to hear what he says.*] Oh. So *that's* it. Play it smart. Go on, see if I care. [CARLING *closes the folder he has been writing in and puts it in a drawer. Then he and* PRUNCHINK *turn and start to walk toward the door.*] Hey! Where the hell do you guys think you're goin'?

Carling [*looking back*]. Don't worry. There'll be an officer along for you in a minute.

Nick [*walking dazedly after them*]. Ya mean you're jus' leavin' me here alone? [NICK *watches in horror as* CARLING *opens the door.*] I could walk outa here. Are you guys crazy? [CARLING *and* PRUNCHINK *go out.*] Hey, you guys. [NICK *grabs hold of the edge of the table and stares at the open door.*] Hey, you guys! I could walk outa here! [He listens for an answer but there is only silence in the room. Slowly he sinks into the chair by the desk.] I could walk outa here. . . .

Curtain.

SING TO ME
THROUGH OPEN WINDOWS

A Play in One Act

CHARACTERS

ANDREW, THE BOY
OTTOMAN, THE MAN
THE CLOWN

SING TO ME
THROUGH OPEN WINDOWS

A Boy *stands alone on a bare stage. Black drapes are hung all around him.*

THE BOY. There are trees around me now. And a stream of shallow water at my feet. The air is cool. A long time ago I was sitting . . . with my friends. [*Music.*] *I think we were in a schoolroom.* But now there are trees around me. And the air is cool.

The black drapes are raised about and behind him. A large, ornate bed slides out. There is someone sleeping in it. A pirate's trunk, rusty and warped, rests on the floor at the foot of the bed. There is a large throne of a chair occupying the opposite side of the room. Also there is a full-length mirror and a tea table beside the bed. An alarm clock sits on the tea table facing away from the bed. Also, a teapot and two teacups. There appears a hint of a door at the rear and a hint of many windows with vines and forest growth tangling over them. THE BOY exits through one of the walls of the room.

The lights now fade. Only a small, faint light remains, illuminating vaguely THE MAN who is sleeping on the bed. There is music. Then that light fades too. The stage is black. But only for a moment. The door at the rear opens silently.

Enter THE CLOWN. He carries a candle. Softly he tiptoes to the bed. Satisfied that its occupant is asleep he walks to the window farthest away and opens it and then the shutters. He looks out and then up at the sky as ribbons of light float into the room. THE CLOWN smiles faintly and walks to the next window. THE MAN in the bed mutters in his sleep and turns over, his back to the spreading light as THE CLOWN goes from window to window, repeating his ritual. THE MAN in the bed turns around again, reaches down for his blankets, and pulls them up over his head. He lies back, completely covered. THE CLOWN opens the last of the windows and stands back proudly, surveying his

work. THE MAN *under the covers emerges. He gazes dazedly*
about the light-flooded room.

The Man. Not only is it unbelievably light in here, it is
also incredibly cold. Close the windows, please.

THE MAN *groans and lies back.* THE CLOWN, *during all*
of this, has not looked at THE MAN *but has, instead, been*
staring out. Now, however, he turns from the windows and
walks over to the bed. He stands, statuelike, peering down
at the buried figure lying before him. Then, after a short
while, he stoops over, lifts gently the edge of the blankets,
and, candle near, peers under them.

The Clown. Time to get up, Ottoman.

THE CLOWN *lets go of the blankets and, snuffing out the*
candle, picks up a golden dressing robe from the floor and
drapes it carefully by the side of the mirror. THE MAN
called OTTOMAN *peers out from his cave of covers.*

Ottoman. I said close the windows. I am freezing to
death.

THE CLOWN *sets a pair of golden slippers by the side of*
the bed.

The Clown. It's the first day of spring.

Ottoman. Nonsense. It's the middle of winter if it's
anything. Now close the windows. I do believe it's about
to snow. [THE CLOWN *shrugs and closes a few of the win-*
dows.] That's better. That's much better. [*He sits up and*
looks around him as if he were seeing the room for the
first time, as if, in fact, he were a stranger there.] Sometimes, Loveless, I wonder what the nature of this madness
is which drives you to opening my windows each miserable,
frigid morning. [THE CLOWN *walks over to the tea table*
and turns the alarm clock toward the man.] Ah, yes. The
middle of the afternoon. Well, it makes no difference. It's
when I always get up. And to me that means morning. I
tell you, Loveless, I need time. Time to acclimatize myself
to the peculiarities of my environment. To the air, the
wind, the special odors of the day. Alas, I am not rugged.
We must admit that fact. But, that fact, once admitted,
gives rise to a most unpleasant suspicion. Which is: that

sometimes, Loveless, I am of the feeling that you open my windows solely in the hope that I might, as a result, contract what constitutes a death of cold. And that suspicion depresses me. [*Short pause.*] Yes, I believe it's about to snow. . . . And I don't like it.

THE CLOWN *watches as the man called* OTTOMAN *rises from his bed and, putting his golden robe about his shoulders, walks to one of the closed windows and stares out, apprehensively. A pause.*

The Clown [*with only the faintest trace of a smile*]. The boy is downstairs, Ottoman. What would you like me to do?

Ottoman. The boy? [*And then, at once comprehending, with alarm.*] The boy! [*Pause, distantly.*] The boy . . . [*Pause.*] Why, is he here so . . . soon? [THE CLOWN *smiles.* OTTOMAN *turns away. He stares out at the cold light of the afternoon in dismay. Music.*] Loveless, what's happening?

The Clown. Happening?

Ottoman. To the seasons. Don't tell me you haven't noticed. The winters—they seem so much longer now; the springs so much colder. I've heard some famous scientists say the earth is tilting, the polar caps are melting, and the climate undergoing a natural change. They assure me that nothing unusual is going on. And yet . . . I wonder. [*Short pause.*] Do you know what I do, first thing in the morning, when I wake up? I look around, that's what I do. I look at my trees and my garden: I look at my house, my clothes, my hands—hands shriveled like the hands of a drowned man. And then I stare at my old dusty mirror and anxiously cross off the days till spring. [*He laughs softly to himself.*] Then, when the big day finally comes, all I can do is sit and wonder. [*Pause.*] Tell me, Loveless. What do you do, first thing in the morning?

The Clown. Why, I go to the toilet, sir, and relieve myself. [THE CLOWN *smiles coldly, bows, and starts to leave.*]

Ottoman. Loveless.

The Clown. Sir?

Ottoman. I think it's time we tried you without your

clown's paint on. I'm getting rather tired of seeing you this way.

The Clown. Just as you wish, Ottoman. I'll find some other costume . . . for tomorrow. [*He stares at* OTTOMAN. *He smiles, then goes out.*]

Music. OTTOMAN *alone. He stares at the door for a moment, then turns and stares at his reflection in the mirror. He stares at first from a distance. Then he approaches it slowly. At last, directly before it, he studies his reflected self. He reaches out and touches it, tentatively. Then he steps back and bows grandly. He now begins to pose before the mirror: a magician rehearsing the studied and aloof grandeur of his life's occupation. Then, for some reason, he stops in the middle of a particularly impressive pose and drops his arms to his side. He smiles sadly. There is a soft knock on the door. The music ends. He turns and stares at the door. Silence. Then another knock, as soft as the first.*

Ottoman. Yes. Come in. [*The door opens. Enter* THE BOY. *He stands in the doorway. Pause.*] Hello, Andrew.

Andrew. Hello, Mr. Jud.

THE BOY *walks into the room.* THE CLOWN *is seen standing behind him in the doorway, smiling slightly.* THE CLOWN *closes the door.*

Ottoman. Please excuse the disorder of my room. You see, I wasn't really . . .

Andrew. That's all right.

Ottoman. . . . Yes. Of course. [*Pause.*] Well. So. Once again. Here you are.

Andrew. Yes, sir.

Ottoman. Been a long time.

Andrew. One year. To the day.

Ottoman. Yes, of course. *To the day.* Somehow, this time, it seemed much longer though. [*He forces a laugh.*] Must have been the weather.

Andrew. Yes, sir.

They both laugh.

Ottoman. And how've you been?

Andrew. Oh, I've been all right.

Ottoman. Ah, splendid.

Andrew. And how have *you* been?

Ottoman. I? Ah, well, you know, the same as ever. Fit as a fiddle, as the old saying goes. [*He laughs.*]

Andrew. I'm glad.

Short pause.

Ottoman. Yes . . . [*Pause.*] Well, what can I get you? Perhaps some tea? A good, brisk cup of tea?

Andrew. No thank you. I'm all right like this.

Ottoman. Yes. Of course. [*Short pause.*] You don't . . . mind if I have some. Do you?

Andrew. No, sir. Please go right ahead.

OTTOMAN *goes to the tea table beside his bed.*

Ottoman. You know . . . [*pours himself a cup of tea*] you took me quite by surprise there. Yes. It's true. Your arrival took me quite by surprise. [*He laughs and sips his tea.*] Ahhh, nothing like a good, strong brew. . . . [*Pause.*] Well, so you've been feeling all right, eh?

Andrew. Yes, sir.

Ottoman. Good. Good to hear. Yes. Good to hear, indeed. [*And he stares out the window and is silent for a while. To himself.*] Why does it feel like winter, though? *That* is what troubles me. [*Staring out through the window still, his eyes dart about, searching. He looks up at the sky.*] . . . Ah, my boy, my boy. I'm afraid it's a bad omen when the seasons start playing tricks.

Andrew. Well, it'll be getting warmer soon. Don't worry.

Ottoman. You think it'll be getting warmer, hm?

Andrew [*laughing*]. It always does.

Silence. Long pause.

Ottoman. Well! Let's have a look at you. What do you say, hm? Let's have ourselves a look. Enough of this chitter-chatter, eh? [*He laughs. Then* THE BOY *laughs.* THE BOY *postures proudly.*] You've grown.

Andrew. Yes, sir!

Ottoman. It . . . looks very good. What is it, an inch? An . . . inch and a half maybe? Yes. An inch and a half. I'd say that was close to the mark.

Andrew [*proudly*]. Two and three-quarter inches, sir. *Exact.*

Ottoman. Two and three-quarter inches. Why . . . why that's almost three. That's . . . a great deal.

Andrew. Yessir. It is. And I've put on weight, too!

Ottoman. A great deal? Why, it's a *very* great deal. Yes. . . . Yes. That's what it is.

Andrew. I've put on weight too, sir.

Ottoman. Yes. A very great deal.

Andrew. Mr. Jud?

Ottoman. And it looks quite good, too. Of course.

Andrew. Mr. Jud? [*Silence.*] Mr. Jud? [OTTOMAN *looks at him, noticing him as if for the very first time.*] I've put on some weight, too.

Ottoman. Oh. Um. Yes. Well, that goes without saying. I mean, add some inches, add some weight, eh? [*He chortles and slaps* ANDREW *on the back.*]

Andrew. Guess how much.

Ottoman. What?

Andrew. Guess how much.

Ottoman. Guess how much *what?*

Andrew. How much weight I've put on.

Ottoman. Ah. How much weight you've put on. Yes. Of course. Well, I . . . don't know. It certainly looks like you've, uh, put on some weight though, doesn't it? Um, have you, in point of fact, put on some weight?

Andrew. Yes, sir. I just told you I did.

Ottoman. Ah yes. Of course. I . . . thought so.

Pause.

Andrew. Well?

Ottoman. Well?

Andrew. Well, guess how much.

Ottoman. Ah. Right. Um. No, I really—— [*He chuckles.*]

Andrew. Oh, please, *guess* how much.

Ottoman. Well, ten . . . fifteen . . . twenty, thirty maybe. I don't know.

Andrew [crestfallen]. Just twelve. That's all.

Ottoman. Just twelve?

Andrew. That's all. Just twelve.

Ottoman. Well! That's not so much, now is it?

Andrew [sadly]. No, sir. I guess not.

Ottoman. Well, I mean, it's good, it's good. Don't get me wrong. Twelve pounds is good. Very good, indeed. It's . . . just not twenty or thirty. If you know what I mean.

Andrew. My father said twelve pounds was a great deal.

Ottoman. And so it is, my boy. A very great deal indeed. It's . . . just not twenty or thirty, that's all. I mean, for instance, to your father twelve pounds is a great deal. To me it's not. That's all. There's no more to the affair than that.

Andrew. My mother said it was a great deal, too.

Ottoman. And so it is, my boy. *So it is.* It's just, you see, that for some reason or another I had . . . well, anticipated the *possibility of more.* [*He laughs.* ANDREW *turns away.*] Well . . . to be perfectly honest with you, my boy . . . I must admit, I suppose, that I had also considered the, um, possibility of less. [OTTOMAN *forces a weak smile.*] There you are. [*He laughs weakly.* ANDREW *grins.*] That please you, does it? [ANDREW *blushes and turns away.* OTTOMAN *stares at him sadly.*] . . . Ah, Andrew, Andrew, when I think back—what was it, three years, four years?

Andrew. Five years, sir. To the day.

Ottoman. Yes. Of course. To the day. *Five years.* Imagine. . . . Oh, how small and frail you were then. And frightened, too. (Not that I can blame you, either.) Lost, like that, way out here in the woods. All those trees hovering over you, animals scuffling about in the dark. And then, as if that weren't bad enough, stumbling, yes, literally stumbling upon this curious, misshapen house of mine sitting oh so nonchalantly in the middle of the forest. Oh yes, my boy, how frightened you were. But yet, how thoroughly excited underneath. Yes. . . . That's what I remember most. How thoroughly excited you were, underneath.

Andrew. Mr. Jud. Next year I graduate from public school.

Ottoman. . . . Hm?

Andrew. Next year I graduate!

Ottoman. What?

Andrew. I've just finished seventh grade and next year I graduate from public school. I'm going to high school then! Even though I don't really want to.

Ottoman [*very distantly*]. What?

The door of the room opens. Enter THE CLOWN, *smiling.*

The Clown. Was there something you wanted, sir?

Ottoman [*very distantly*]. What?

The Clown. I thought I heard you call.

Ottoman. I . . . did not call.

The Clown. Forgive me. But I could have sworn you did.

Ottoman [*distantly*]. I . . . did not call.

The Clown. Forgive me. [*He begins to back out of the room.*]

Ottoman. You know very *well* I didn't call!

The Clown. Forgive me, sir. [*He backs into the doorway, smiling.*] Forgive me. [*He closes the door.*]

Short pause. OTTOMAN *runs to the door and flings it open. He stares through the empty door and down the empty hallway. Long pause. At last he closes the door and turns back into the room, slowly. He glances fleetingly at* THE BOY.

Then he walks slowly to the table.

Ottoman. Well, how about some tea? Yes. How's that for an idea? A good brisk cup of tea. [OTTOMAN, *having filled his cup, now lifts it delicately and savors its contents. His hand is trembling slightly.*] Ah, nothing like a good strong brew. [*He stares out a window.*]

Andrew. Mr. Jud? Mr. Jud, there's something I have to tell you. That is, actually it's something I've come to ask you to . . . do for me. If you will. Mr. Jud, I've been——

Ottoman [*distantly*]. Andrew . . .

Andrew. Hm?

Ottoman [*distantly*]. Andrew Linden . . .

Andrew. Yes, sir?

Ottoman [*not conscious of* THE BOY'S *presence*]. Now there's a name for you, Andrew Linden. Andrewlinden. . . . *Andrew* . . . *Linden.* Yes, there's a name for you. A beautiful name. A truly beautiful name. [*And then, for the first time, he becomes aware of* THE BOY'S *presence.*] Tell me. What is your father's name?

Andrew. Mr. Linden.

Ottoman. No, no. His *first* name. What is your father's *first* name?

Andrew. Harry.

Ottoman [*greatly disappointed*]. Oh. [*Pause.*] Well then, from now on you must call him Harold. That's *much finer!* [*And then he turns to the window again and stares far, far out.*]

Andrew. Mr. Jud?

OTTOMAN *turns and smiles to* THE BOY. *He puts back his teacup.*

Ottoman. I'm sorry. Forgive me. I must have drifted off somewhere. . . . *Well.* Time for the show! What shall it be today? The Dark Ages, prehistory, the Middle East? The Far East? Say Hong Kong? Yes. Say, perchance, *Hong Kong.* A place fabulous beyond your wildest dreams. A vast and desolate valley of ruined temples and palaces, an Oriental sepulcher, a landscape, yes, Andrew, a landscape of a civilization long lost. Now how does that sound? [*Silence.*] Hm . . . Well then, perhaps not a story at all. Perhaps, today, you'd prefer to start with——

Andrew. A trick!

Ottoman. Yes. A trick. A trick no mortal has ever seen before! A——

Andrew. Yes, that one! Show me that one again!

Ottoman. Ah, *that* one. You want to see *that* one?

Andrew. Yessir!

Ottoman. Very well then. I'll show it! That trick *so*

daring, so unusual that once again you will be left gasping in wonderment, in dismay, in open disbelief that so strange a thing could actually occur. I trust you are ready?

Andrew. Yes, sir!

Ottoman. Good. Then I take great pleasure in presenting, Ottoman the Great, Master Magician: Man of a Thousand Disguises, Man of a Thousand Tricks! [ANDREW *applauds wildly.*] Thank you. Thank you. [*He moves quickly to the treasure chest and opens it.* ANDREW *rises slightly from his chair, trying to peek inside.* OTTOMAN *stares for a brief moment into the mysterious trunk, then like a hungry bird swoops down into it and scoops out a large red box with yellow and green butterflies drawn on its sides. With the same gesture he closes the trunk.*] We see before us a box with nothing in it. Witness. [*He flourishes the box through the air, opens a snap, thrusts his arm through it, and shows it to be quite empty.*] That is, my friends, an ordinary box to anyone but Ottoman the Great. For to Ottoman the impossible is the commonplace. Thus, with a sweep of the cloak . . . [*reaches into his pocket and takes out an old wrinkled handkerchief and sweeps it before the box*] and a rap of the cane . . . [*raps the box with his index finger*] we have . . . *presto!* A hat! [*And from the box he draws a large silk topper.* ANDREW *gasps and claps his hands.* OTTOMAN *bows and smiles.*] Ah, but that is not all. For from the hat I now produce . . . [*passes the handkerchief magically above the brim*] a rabbit! [ANDREW *rises and stares, dumbfounded, at the large, limp, mangy, moth-eaten rabbit held by its neck ever so delicately in the magician's hand.* OTTOMAN *bows to his left and his right as if applause were coming from all about him.*] Thank you, ladies and gentlemen. I thank you all.

Andrew [*cautiously*]. Mr. Jud?

Ottoman. I thank you, one and all. You've been so kind.

Andrew. Mr. Jud . . .

Ottoman. Bless you. Bless you.

OTTOMAN *throws the unseen audience kisses. He bows to*

the unheard ovation. ANDREW *tugs hesitantly on his sleeve.*

Andrew. Mr. Jud.

Ottoman. Yes, my son? What is it?

Andrew. Mr. Jud . . . That rabbit is dead.

Pause.

Ottoman [*softly, distantly*]. What?

Andrew. I think that rabbit is dead.

Ottoman. Why . . . why, Andrew, I'm surprised at you. To say a thing like that. [*He drops the rabbit into the hat.*] Of course it's not dead. It's . . . stunned, that's all. Simply stunned. I mean, wouldn't *you* be stunned if you found *yourself*, suddenly, inside a hat?

Andrew [*laughing*]. How could I get inside a hat? I'm too *big.*

Ottoman. Ah, but that is the point, my boy. You forget, I'm a magician. *That is the point.* [*He smiles and bows grandly. He strides over to the trunk and opens it. He dumps the rabbit out of the hat and watches it fall. Then he drops the hat and the red box with the butterflies on it. He stares down at them. Enter* THE CLOWN, *smiling. The magician senses his presence. He looks up from the trunk and whirls around.*] What are you doing here?

The Clown. You mean you didn't call?

And then they stare at one another, THE CLOWN *still smiling, the magician frozen with fear.* THE BOY *wanders near the open and now unguarded trunk in an attempt to peek inside. The magician spots him.*

Ottoman. Get away from there! [*Rushing back, he slams the lid.*] You're not supposed to look in there. I've—I've told you that before! Why—— [*And then he realizes that he's shouting. So he says more softly.*] Why—— [*And then still more softly, feigning calmness.*] Why, a trunk like this, my boy, is—is no . . . ordinary trunk, Hu-ho, no! It's a, uh, *magician's* trunk! Which means, of course, it's filled with . . . the secrets of his . . . magic. Which means its, um, *privacy* must . . . be respected. Though I think I've . . . told you . . . that before. . . . [*He stares at* THE BOY, *lost in some distant thought. Suddenly he remembers* THE CLOWN. *He whirls on him. Sotto voce.*] What do you want here?

The Clown. I thought you called.

Ottoman. I did not call.

The Clown. I'm sorry, but I thought you did.

Ottoman. I did not call!

The Clown. Ah well, forgive me, sir, but you see I thought you did.

Ottoman. You know very *well* I didn't call!

The Clown [*laughing it off*]. I'm sorry, sir. I thought you did.

Ottoman [*softly*]. Get out.

The Clown. Well, maybe there's something you want, anyway.

Ottoman. Get out of here.

The Clown. Some more tea perhaps.

Ottoman. I said *get out of here!*

The Clown. Another rabbit?

Ottoman. Leave me *alone!*

The Clown. But of course you do get my point.

Ottoman. Leave me alone!

The Clown. I mean, after all, sir, why waste a trip? That's what I mean.

THE CLOWN *grins at the magician. A pause.*

Ottoman. I am vanishing, Andrew. Suddenly, I am vanishing. . . .

Stretching his arms above him, THE CLOWN *sweeps a circle through the air. The light in the room changes: a spot of light falls on the center of the floor and all the rest darkens.* THE CLOWN *mimes the movements of a drummer. A drum roll is heard. Then suddenly he stops. The drum roll stops, too. Carnival music heard.*

The Clown. Introducing! For your pleasure! "The Animals!" [*Whereupon* THE CLOWN *springs with a growl and, landing on all fours, sniffs the air.*]

Ottoman [*to* ANDREW]. When you're not here, you see, we . . . often play a little game. He pretends he's some circus performer, and I . . . the ringmaster. It—what can I say?—*amuses* us. Although, for some reason, it always seems to amuse him more than me. Even though I . . . always win. [*He laughs at this.* THE CLOWN *growls and claws the air.*] As you can see he, um, would like to play it now. [*And again he laughs.*] A, uh . . . [*Growl from* THE CLOWN.] "command performance" for *you*, so to speak.

Whereupon OTTOMAN *pulls the sash from his robe and raises it above him like a whip.* THE CLOWN *growls angrily. But for some reason the magician does not strike, but, instead, slowly lowers his arm and stares at the sash.*

The Clown [*softly*]. Ottoman.

Ottoman. I don't feel like playing.

The Clown. Ottoman.

Ottoman. I'm sorry but I don't feel like playing. Perhaps tomorrow.

OTTOMAN *starts to put the sash back on his robe.* THE CLOWN *springs through the air, roaring. He grabs at* OTTOMAN's *throat. They tumble to the floor. But the magician manages to fling* THE CLOWN *away long enough to draw back his sash and strike* THE CLOWN. *He whips him mercilessly.* THE CLOWN *crawls off, whimpering. The magician stares at his sash, then at* THE BOY *for a moment, then looks away. He puts the sash back on.*

The Clown [*reappearing suddenly from the shadows*]. The tightrope walker comes next, *if I recall.*

Ottoman [*softly*]. I don't want to play any more. I've decided.

The Clown. Announcing——

Ottoman. I said I *don't want to play this game.*

The Clown. "The Tightrope Walker!"

THE CLOWN *mimes a drum roll. A drum roll is heard. He begins to mime the act of climbing. The drum roll continues.*

Ottoman. Look! Did you hear what I said? [*But* THE CLOWN *doesn't answer. He simply continues climbing. At last he reaches the top. The drum roll ceases. He looks down. To him now the ground is way below. Music. He looks over at the place he must reach.* OTTOMAN *is standing there.* THE CLOWN *smiles coldly and cautiously begins his trip. One foot after the other he balances his way along the wire.*] I don't enjoy this game. [THE CLOWN *stops walking.*] I want to stop. [OTTOMAN *turns and starts to walk away.*]

The Clown. Ottoman! [*The magician looks back.* THE CLOWN, *grinning wildly, his arms oustretched, his fingers grasping, sprints along the wire toward his prey.* OTTOMAN *rushes back and, pretending his fingers are scissors, snips the invisible wire.* THE CLOWN *opens his mouth as if in screaming and, in slow motion, mimes the act of falling. Down and down he spins to the floor below. His body lands, twisted in a grotesque heap.* OTTOMAN *laughs and claps his hands.* THE CLOWN *looks up from the floor.*] Almost got to you that time. [OTTOMAN *stops laughing.* THE CLOWN *gets up.*] Best I've ever died. [*And so saying, he hobbles off into the shadows.*]

OTTOMAN *stares at* THE BOY. THE CLOWN *reappears with a small black box. He sets it in the middle of the room and steps back proudly.* OTTOMAN *looks away from* THE BOY *and sees the box.*

Ottoman. That's not the right box!

The Clown. I beg your pardon?

Ottoman. That box. It's not the right box.

The Clown. Of course it's the right box. Announcing! "The Incredible *Disappearing Man!*"

Ottoman. I tell you that's not the right box!

THE CLOWN *opens it.*

The Clown. You don't know what you're talking about.

Having opened it, THE CLOWN *stands back proudly. He mimes the drum roll. Drum roll heard. Then music again.*

Ottoman [*staring into the box*]. It's too small!

The Clown. Too *small?*

Ottoman. You'll never fit.

The Clown. I've always fitted in the past.

Ottoman. You've switched boxes, that's what.

The Clown. Announcing . . . "The Incredible *Disappearing Man!"*

And THE CLOWN *steps into the box. He looks up at the magician for a moment and smiles. Then he begins his contortions, his attempts to squeeze himself into the small black space.*

Ottoman. Come here, Andrew. Give us a hand.

Andrew. Mr. Jud, must he do this?

Ottoman. Of—of *course* he must do it! He's begun, hasn't he?

They push. THE CLOWN *squeezes. The box bursts open at the seams.* OTTOMAN *stares at the spectacle in horror.* THE CLOWN *gets up from the floor. He gathers the pieces.*

The Clown [*shrugging*]. Always *used* to work . . . [*He chuckles and starts to leave.*]

Ottoman. Well, maybe if you started exercising! [*The* CLOWN *stops at this and looks back.*] Lost a little weight; limbered up a bit. Must be . . . years since you've . . . done . . . any . . . exercising.

The Clown. Five years, sir. To the day. [*And smiling coldly, he walks off into the shadows.*]

The magician stares dazedly away. Pause. From the shadows now appears a most curious object—a person covered by a huge, dark, and somewhat tattered blanket. Since not even the feet of this person can be seen, it gives the impression of a huge mole moving across the floor. It stops behind the magician.

Andrew. Mr. Jud!

OTTOMAN *turns around. He does not seem surprised. If anything, he seems saddened.*

Ottoman [to ANDREW]. It's only him. Don't be afraid. [*He lifts the bottom of the blanket.* THE CLOWN's *feet can be seen.* OTTOMAN *drops the edge of the blanket.*] He wants, you see, to play "The Clown." Since, however, he's already *dressed* as a clown, he covers himself with this mangy blanket, believing that in this way his act will retain its element of surprise. [OTTOMAN *laughs, but weakly.* THE BOY *laughs too. The blanket moves into the spotlight.*] Introducing for your amusement . . . for your laughter . . . "The Clown." [*Distantly.*] What *clown?* . . . [*Music. A cacophony of carnival noises. It grows louder and louder.* THE CLOWN *pulls his blanket off. He is staring at* OTTOMAN, *no sign of emotion visible on his painted face.* OTTOMAN *turns and sees him.*] No. . . . No! No! No-o-o-o-o! You're not doing it *right!* You're—you're . . . you're not—you're not supposed to . . . to look at . . . me. [*But* THE CLOWN *continues to stare.*] I said you're *not supposed to look at meeeeee!* [*And then* THE CLOWN *smiles slightly, turns, and walks briskly from the room. The magician stares after him. The music fades. Silence. The lights come back up.*] You're supposed to . . . [*And then he turns and stares at* THE BOY. *Pause.*] Usually it, uh, goes somewhat better. Our . . . little game. [*The magician forces a laugh. And then he turns and walks to one of his windows. He stares far out.*]

Music: *vague and somewhere far away. The colors of the room now seem to change. Suddenly it is dusk and the dying light of the day drifts softly in, washing the room in pale shadows.*

. .*Andrew.* Now in looking back on all of this a great many years from now I will realize that it was at *this very moment* that I suddenly began to remember what it was I had come here to do and to say. And all of this while the magician stood at his window staring out, the tallest shadow in a room full of shadows and ghosts, full of sounds and wind.

When *the magician speaks, his voice will also be heard from somewhere in the far distance, echoing, the words almost too vague to understand.*

Ottoman *and* Distant Voice of Ottoman [*together*]. I met him years ago. Somewhat like I met you. That is, he met me. By accident. He is——

OTTOMAN's *own voice now stops, though his lips will move*

as his words are heard echoing in the distance.

Distant Voice of Ottoman. . . . not a clown.

Andrew. And then I remember. But strangely. For the words I remember are like the words of an unfamiliar language. And although I say them, some time later I will ask myself, *Now what was it again that you said to him . . . back there?* [*The magician turns sharply from the window.*] Which was when he turned so sharply from the window and said, "What?" with that wild, lost look in his eyes. And said, "What? . . . *What?*"

Distant Voice of Ottoman. You mean you want to stay here?

Andrew. And the boy said yes, he wanted to stay there. He said no, he did not want to go home ever again. And then the magician asked him

Andrew and *Distant voice of Ottoman* [*together*]. Why? . . . Why? . . . Why?

Andrew. But this the boy was ready for—because he knew that this was why he was there in the first place. "I don't like it at home as much as I like it here," he said. "They're nice but they don't let me do what I really want. For instance, they would never understand about you." And that was all the boy said. And he truly believed it would be enough. [*The magician is staring into his mirror. He turns slowly and walks toward* THE BOY.] The magician is turned now and is walking very slowly. He is getting larger. Now a pair of hands is reaching out, hands shriveled like the hands of a drowned man, and they are touching a pair of shoulders, lightly. And someone is saying, "Andrew Linden.". . .

Andrew, Ottoman, and *Distant voice of Ottoman* [*together*]. Andrew Linden . . .

Ottoman and *Distant voice of Ottoman* [*together*]. Andrew Linden . . .

Ottoman [*distantly*]. Andrew Linden . . . [*Pause.*] Now there's a name for you. Andrewlinden . . . *Andrew—Linden.* Yes, there's a name for you. A beautiful name. A truly beautiful name.

Andrew. And then the boy feels the soft pressure of those hands which are still touching him and he knows at that moment that he will soon be gone from there and will not see the magician again, ever again. And that was when he heard himself saying, "I love you, Mr. Jud, I love you"; and he was perplexed by that, for although he had come truly wanting to stay he had not come expecting to hear himself say that. Although he knew at that moment that it was true. Just as he will also know it, later on.

Ottoman [*softly*]. It's getting late now. I think you'd better go before it gets too dark.

Andrew [*softly, distantly*]. Yes. . . . [*But for the moment neither of them moves. They simply stand, THE BOY in front of the magician, two shadows in a quickly darkening room. The magician's hands are on THE BOY's shoulders still.*] And then they go.

The two of them now walk to the door, the magician with his arm around THE BOY. They pause at the door. And then the door opens. THE BOY leaves. For a while the magician stares at the door. Then he turns slowly away. He walks to the mirror and stares into it, so distantly that it is almost as if he were staring through it. Music is heard. Suddenly he runs to the bell cord and pulls on it madly.

Ottoman [*desperately*]. Loveless! [*He pulls on the bell cord again violently.*] Loveless!! Where are you!? Where are you?

The door opens. Enter THE CLOWN, smiling.

The Clown. You called me, sir?

Ottoman. Tell him to come back!

The Clown. I beg your pardon?

Ottoman. The boy, you fool. Tell him to come back.

The Clown. I'm sorry to disappoint you, sir, but that will be impossible.

Ottoman [*weakly*]. What . . . do you mean?

The Clown. I mean, he is gone.

Short pause.

Ottoman. You—you mean he . . . didn't wait? I, I thought certainly he'd . . . wait. At least a little while. You know in . . . case something happened.

The Clown. No, sir. He left at once.

Ottoman. I don't believe you. You're lying.

The Clown. No, sir, I'm not. The boy is gone. [*Pause.*] Sir, I don't wish to seem impertinent, but if I may offer a suggestion. [OTTOMAN *turns to him sharply, a dazed and beaten look on his face.*] It might have something to do with the storm.

Ottoman [*fearfully*]. What storm?

The Clown. Why, the snowstorm, sir. It has started to snow. [OTTOMAN *walks dazedly to the window and stares out. Wind begins to blow into the room, making the curtains fly like pennants.*] He might have wanted to get home before the heavy snow began to fall.

Ottoman [*not listening*]. Spring, Loveless. What's happened to it? Soon the ground and the rivers and the trees will all be sleeping under white sheets. Snow can be so beautiful, Loveless. And sometimes, it can be so . . . [THE CLOWN *starts to leave.*] No. . . . No, don't go just yet. There are certain things we must first look after.

The Clown. Yes, sir?

Ottoman. If you would, Loveless, I'd like you to draw the shades and lock the windows, fasten the shutters and bolt the doors. In short, close up the house. There's nothing more to be done here.

The Clown. I don't understand.

Ottoman. You understand perfectly well. I know.

The Clown. Sir, I——

Ottoman [*with a sad laugh*]. Never mind. Have it your way then. Loveless, tell me . . . have you ever wondered what happens to someone when he falls asleep? *Tell me.*

The Clown. No, sir.

Ottoman. You mean you've never wondered what goes on around you, while your eyes are shut?

The Clown. No, sir.

Ottoman. Of course you have. Everyone has. . . . Including me. Well, do you know what I used to think?

The Clown. No, sir. What is that?

Ottoman. I used to think . . . that *you* were watching me.

The Clown. I?

Ottoman. Yes, you. Now isn't that foolish?

The Clown. Sir, I——

Ottoman. It's all right, Loveless. I apologize. For, you see, I know now that it wasn't *really* you. Loveless, it's cold in here. Have you closed all the windows?

The Clown. No, sir. I was just about to. Should I——

Ottoman. Never mind. It doesn't matter. Listen, Loveless. Listen to me. *Fear.* Remember that word. You think you know what it means but you never do. It's something like regret. Fear is like regret. Only with fear there's not much time left.

The Clown. I——

Ottoman. Listen. Don't interrupt. I am afraid, Loveless . . . for I know now that it wasn't really you but someone else. That all my life it was someone else, standing there in the dark, watching me . . . and laughing. [*Pause.*] I have vanished, Loveless. Suddenly I have vanished. [*And then the magician slumps forward in his velvet chair, his eyes falling shut.*]

THE CLOWN *stands for a moment, motionless, then walks over to the magician and lifts him in his arms. He carries the lifeless body slowly over to the trunk and gently lowers it in. And then he closes the lid.* THE CLOWN *stares far out into what is now the night as snowflakes fall through the windows and into the room.*

And then the room begins to disappear. Its parts slide slowly into the shadows just as they had originally slid from the shadows into the light. THE CLOWN *stands beside the trunk and slowly fades with that portion of the room. He passes* THE BOY. THE BOY *has been in the shadows, hidden, unseen. But now as the room dissolves he moves forward, watching the slow, mechanical process. He stares at* THE CLOWN *as* THE CLOWN *slides past. He stares down at the trunk. And then the room is* gone. *The stage, once more, is bare except for the black curtains around it; except for the flashing white spots of falling snow. The music fades.* THE BOY *walks offstage, unhurriedly as*

The curtain falls.

THE HERO

A Pantomime

CHARACTERS

The Man
The Woman

THE HERO

Curtain rises. A large screen is seen. It reads: "THE HERO." The screen rises.

Desert. Sun not yet up. In the background, gray cyclorama. Pause. Sun now starts to rise, slowly. The sun is a bright, orange disk which is hoisted, by a wire, up the cyclorama. As it climbs, the light on the stage grows stronger. Sun up. Intense light. Long pause.

Enter a Man, *stage left. He is in rags. He carries a well-looked-after attaché case. He stumbles from exhaustion and falls. He sits up, laughs at his fall, dusts himself off, sighs, and mops the perspiration from his brow. He carefully dusts off his attaché case. Pause. He searches the ground beside him. He looks back up. Pause. He looks back in the direction from whence he's come. Pause. He searches the ground. He looks back up. Short pause. He leaps up and runs off, stage left. Long pause.*

Re-enter The Man, *stage left. He drags behind him a huge eight-foot scroll, tightly rolled. He comes back to his spot in the desert and sits. He puts his scroll and attaché case next to each other and pats them both affectionately. He now takes a sandwich out of his pocket and a salt shaker as well. He sprinkles salt on the sandwich, wets his lips in anticipation, and bites. The sandwich is rock-hard. He tries to bite again, undaunted by his first failure and his sore teeth. He bites again. No use. He bangs it against the attaché case. This does no good either. So he shrugs, laughs weakly, and puts the sandwich down to bake in the sun.*

He sighs. Reflects. Remembers. Reaches into a pocket. Nothing. Tries the other pocket. Pulls out a large map. Holds it up before him. Its title: "MAP OF THE WORLD." He sighs sadly. It is quite obvious that a good part of the map is missing. He rises. He examines the place he is inhabiting at the moment. He checks on the map. He finds it. He smiles. The smile disappears. He puts his finger on the corresponding spot on the map. He gazes back in the direction from whence he's come. He sighs. He rips off another section of the map. He tosses it away, smiling sadly. He folds the rest of the map up neatly and puts it back in his pocket. He sighs. He sits.

He jumps back up, staring off, stage right. Something seen in the distance. He peers. Then reaches into his pocket and pulls out a pair of opera glasses. He gazes through them. Then he takes them away from his eyes and blows the dust off. He peers again. He lets them fall to the sand. In his excitement the opera glasses are now forgotten.

He runs to his attaché case, opens it, thinks twice, closes it. Runs instead to his scroll. Lifts it up. Sets one pole in the sand left of stage center, unrolls the scroll and sets the other pole in the sand right of center. The scroll is blank. The appearance given is that of a makeshift billboard. The bottom of the billboard touches the sand. The top is well above his head.

Now he gets the attaché case. He brings it over, opens it up. Paintbox inside. He goes, gets the opera glasses, blows the dust off, checks the distance again, drops the glasses, rushes to the paintbox. Begins to paint.

What he paints—or better, sketches—is an oasis, a palm tree in the middle, a cool, clear, green pool of water beside the tree, a tall mountain in the distance. And on the other side of the tree, a blanket with wine, grapes, and bread spread out on it. He closes the paintbox, hides it behind the billboard. He runs back, picks up the opera glasses, checks, puts them down, smooths his hair, straightens his general appearance, and sits under the shade of the palm tree. He whistles casually.

Enter a WOMAN, *stage right. She is in rags. She stops, stunned by the sudden appearance of an oasis. She studies it for a few moments. And* THE MAN, *of course, as well.* THE MAN *pays her no attention. He simply whistles to himself. She struts slowly past, pretending not to notice. She studies the scene from the corner of her eye. Once past, she checks behind the billboard. Sees, of course, nothing. She looks into the distance. Sees, of course, nothing.*

While her back is turned, THE MAN *flips his opera glasses next to her feet. She notices them. Smile of discovery. She picks them up, looks through, takes them away, blows the dust off, looks through again. In all directions she sees, of course, nothing. She frowns. She tosses the glasses away.*

THE MAN *starts to whistle again. She stares at him. She ponders. She goes then beside the billboard where he can't see her. She smoothes her hair, straightens herself up, as best she can.*

She reappears, smiling. She nods her greeting. He rises. He offers her his place under the palm tree. She smiles her gracious acceptance. She sits. He sits next to her. She nods to him. He nods to her. Pause.

He casually reaches back under the billboard and pulls, from behind it, his sandwich. Smiling, he offers her the sandwich. Smiling, she accepts. She moistens her lips. She bites. He looks away slightly, so as not to embarrass her when: she can't manage to bite the thing. She checks him from the corner of her eye, sees he's not watching, and bites again. No use. She bangs it against her knee. The sandwich cracks in half. She stares at it, dumbfounded. Then she picks up the two pieces and offers him one. She smiles her thanks. He takes the other half, smiling casually. As soon as he does, he turns slightly and examines it, amazed.

Suddenly she touches his shoulder and he turns. He looks at her. She motions to the surrounding oasis and sighs, with pleasure. She laughs warmly. He laughs modestly. They snuggle up to each other. They stare off into the distance, smiles on their faces. Long pause.

The orange disk of the sun sets slowly against the cyclorama. The lights fade as it does. They snuggle more, as the cold of night approaches. The vague smiles on their faces never leave. Indeed, they almost seem frozen there. Darkness.

Slow curtain.

THE CONQUEST OF EVEREST

A Divertissement

CHARACTERS

ALMENSIDE, *a young woman*
ALMANSTAR, *a young man*
THE CHINESE SOLDIER

SCENE—Mount Everest.

THE CONQUEST OF EVEREST

*Seen is the peak of Mount Everest, peeking through a
cloud. Most of the stage is covered by this cloud. Silence.
Then, after a while, a slight scraping sound is heard. Rocks
tumble. People approach, but remain hidden from view
while speaking the lines that follow.*

ALMENSIDE. Hurry, Mr. Almanstar, or we'll miss the sunset!

Almanstar. Can't hear you!

Almenside. The sunset! I'm afraid we're going to miss
the *sunset!*

Almanstar. Wait a minute. [*Sound of rocks tumbling.*]
Damned ice! Ah. Here we are. Made it. What?

Almenside. I said if we don't shake a leg, Mr. Almanstar, we're going to miss the sunset. And after all the
trouble it's taken to climb up here, wouldn't *that* make
a fine kettle of fish.

Almanstar. Miss Almenside.

Almenside [*crossly*]. What?

Almanstar. I have not climbed all this distance *just* to
see the sun.

Almenside. You haven't?

Almanstar. I've wished *also* to see you. By the way, are
you finding it somewhat . . . hard to breathe?

Almenside. Mr. Almanstar.

Almanstar. Doesn't seem to . . . be much *air,* up here.
[*He chuckles.*]

Almenside. Mr. *Almanstar!*

Almanstar. Yo.

Almenside. I think it's time you *got something straight.*

Almanstar. Pardon?

Almenside. In a very few moments, God willing, we
shall be sitting on the top of a very tall mountain in a
rather remote corner of the earth. Well. I don't know
what sort of girl you think I am, but all I can say is, *don't
mess around.*

Almanstar. I think my hands are turning blue.

Almenside. Longer climb than we'd thought.

Almanstar. I know. Should have brought gloves.

Almenside. Well! Back to what we were saying. Mr. Almanstar, I like you. Let's make no bones about it. I like your spirit, your derring-do. Most men, most American men, I find lackluster, snivelly, and sickly. You, however, seem willing to take that certain adventurous plunge which always, in the past, has distinguished the real, *true* man.

Almanstar. Well, what can I say? I like to think that *no* man would have let a young lady undertake a treacherous ascent like this, all alone. [*He chortles.*]

Almenside. Nevertheless, despite your protests, Mr. Almanstar, the fact is that in this sorry day and age *spirit,* such as yours, is rare.

Almanstar. If that's true, Miss Almenside, then surely it's no rarer than your *own.*

Almenside. Why, thank you. [*Short pause.*] Mr. Almanstar. Would you kindly remove your hand from the calf of my right leg?

Almanstar. Sorry. Didn't mean to be fresh. But I'm afraid I was slipping. [*Slight avalanche sound.*] Ah, here we are. All right now.

Almenside. To continue: while it's true that I've grown somewhat fond of you, nevertheless—and here's the point I was trying just now to make—this fact does not entitle you to liberties.

Almanstar. Liberties?

Almenside. Mr. Almanstar, what do you say we quit fooling around? I am wearing, as you well have seen, a rather *full skirt.* I have asked you before; I will ask you only *one more time:* would you mind climbing *ahead* of me? I'm not the sort who goes in for giving strange men a . . . "free show." [*Rocks tumble.*] Thank you.

ALMANSTAR's *hand breaks through the top of the cloud. It gropes about, then disappears.*

Almanstar. I think we're almost there.

Almenside. Well, I certainly should hope so. We've been climbing for at *least* five hours.

Almanstar. Lucky we found that path. I suspect this
thing could have taken even *longer.* [*He chortles.*]
Whoops, there go those rocks again.

Landslide sound.

Almenside. Mr. Almanstar, do you really think it was
wise, not wearing shoes?

Almanstar. Of course. Toughens the feet. One must
toughen the feet at every chance. The trouble with the
world today, Miss Almenside, if you don't mind my saying
so, is that people have grown soft! Now back in Stamford
where I teach phys. ed. we have the kids run——

Almenside. Mr. Almanstar!

Almanstar. Hm?

Almenside. Don't you think it's time we made, as they
say, "the final push"?

Almanstar. Guess you're right. May I have the rope?

Almenside. You may have the rope.

Almanstar. Well then, "Around the horn we go!" [*Now
they are both right below the top of the cloud, so when
ALMANSTAR starts to twirl his lariat—for that is what it is
—the noose waves way above the mountain's summit. He
pokes his head up to see what's wrong.*] Hey! We're *there.*
ALMENSIDE *appears through the top of the cloud. They
both gaze about in ecstasy.*

Almenside. God.

Almanstar. Pretty.

Long pause.

Almenside. Well, what do we do *now?*

Almanstar. Guess we start back down.

Almenside. Seems like there should be something more.

Almanstar. Could take pictures.

Almenside. Ah, *there* you are!

Almanstar [*laughing*]. Alley-oop! [*He gives her a boost.
She rises from the cloud and sits on an edge of the peak.
She is wearing a summer frock and is barefoot. She carries
a purse. Now ALMANSTAR climbs up. He is wearing Florida
garb and is, of course, barefoot. He decides to balance himself on the peak.*] Hello, World!

ALMANSTAR *chortles. He falls off the peak and disappears into the cloud. Loud avalanche sound.*

Almenside [*peering into the cloud*]. Mr. Almanstar, are you all right?

Silence. Then a hand gropes up through the cloud. AL-MANSTAR *struggles back into view.*

Almanstar. Had a little fall there.

Almenside. You'd better not try that again.

Almanstar. Damned ice, gets a little slippery. [*He laughs, sits beside her.*] Got your camera?

Almenside. Yup. [*She reaches into her purse and takes out a Brownie box camera.*] Hold this please?

ALMANSTAR *takes it, examines it.*

Almanstar. Cute li'l thing.

Almenside [*searching through her purse*]. Know I had some film. I'm always forgetting the film. Ah, here we are. [*She takes a roll of film out of her purse. In doing so, however, she drops her purse into the cloud. She peers over into the cloud. He peers too.*] Oh, well. I'll get it on the way down. [*She examines the film.*] . . . "Do not load in sunlight." [*She gazes about in distress. Then she reaches over to* ALMANSTAR *and reclaims her camera.*] Be right back.

ALMENSIDE *descends into the cloud.* ALMANSTAR *gazes about, twiddles his thumbs.*

Almanstar [*calling down to her*]. Must be a pretty tall mountain. Seems higher than any of the other peaks. [*He laughs. He does not notice when a ladder rises through the cloud to his left. He takes a sandwich out of his pocket and starts to eat.*] Climb like this makes a man *real* hungry.

While ALMANSTAR *is munching, a* CHINESE SOLDIER *appears above the cloud. He wears an oxygen mask and carries a machine gun. He grips the ladder nervously. Also, he clings nervously to a huge banner that clearly he'd planned to plant on the peak. The banner says,* "CON-QUERORS OF EVEREST." THE CHINESE SOLDIER *stares at* ALMANSTAR *in dismay. He climbs back down the ladder. The ladder descends.*

Meanwhile, ALMANSTAR, *who has also been sipping a Coke, tosses the bottle off to his left and into the cloud. A loud* KLONK *is heard.* THE CHINESE SOLDIER *reappears.*

The Chinese Soldier. 壹大己求处扌！ [ALMANSTAR *turns in surprise.* THE SOLDIER *lifts forth a broken Coke bottle. Angrily.*] 遑鼎大...！

Almanstar [*bending over and peering into the cloud*]. Hey! Come on up here.

Almenside [*still out of sight*]. What is it? [*She appears.*] Oh! How *nice.*

The Chinese Soldier [*waving the Coke bottle angrily*]. 疟扌日大龙

Almenside. Now hold still. [*She aims the camera at him. When he realizes what she's doing, he removes his oxygen mask and smiles. She snaps the picture.*] Thank you.

The smile on his face fades. He holds out his hand.

The Chinese Soldier. 哭虫孚

ALMANSTAR *reaches into his pocket, takes out a coin, and tosses it to* THE SOLDIER. THE SOLDIER *catches it, examines it, then puts on his oxygen mask and descends. The ladder disappears from view.*

Almenside. How much you give him?

Almanstar. Half dollar.

Almenside. Quarter would have done. Don't want to spoil them, you know.

Almanstar. Miss Almenside . . . ?

ALMANSTAR *grabs her and kisses her. After a few moments, they break. She turns quickly from him. Pause.*

Almenside. You don't happen to have another sandwich, do you, Mr. Almanstar?

Almanstar. You can . . . have the rest of *this* one. [*He gives it to her.* ALMENSIDE *takes it, eyes averted. She eats. Long silence. Suddenly.*] I hope you don't—— Well, I hope you didn't . . .

Almenside. I'm *sure* you forgot the salt.

ALMANSTAR *hands her some salt.*

Almanstar. I'm sorry about that little incident. Just now. I was, well——

Almenside. I think it's probably best if we don't discuss it. [*She eats her sandwich.*] Hm. Getting a little nippy.

Almanstar. Here! Take my jacket. [*He takes off and gives her his tropical jacket. His shirt has short sleeves.*]

Almenside. Don't suppose it's going to snow, do you?

Almanstar. Miss Almenside, I *must* explain! That kiss——

Almenside. Is already forgotten. [*She hands back the salt.*] Thank you for the salt.

Almanstar. You seemed to *enjoy* it all right! While it was *going on!*

Almenside. Mountain air, Mr. Almanstar.

Almanstar. Mountain air?

Almenside. Is notorious. One must never trust the emotions it engenders. Ever done any scuba diving?

Almanstar. Game to try, though.

Almenside. Last summer. Off Las Palmas in the Grand Canaries. Went down a hundred-fifty feet. Nitrogen narcosis. "Rapture of the depths." Fell in love with a flounder. . . . Same thing as here.

Almanstar. Are you comparing me to a——

Almenside. I'm only saying, Mr. Almanstar, that there are times when a girl must stay on her guard—emotion-wise. And you are quickly becoming an emotional risk.

Almanstar. You're fond of me.

Almenside. We have *much* in *common.* . . . [*Pause.*] If you like, we *could* hold hands. [*They hold hands.*] Actually, another kiss might not hurt. [*They kiss. It is a long kiss.*] Actually—funny thing is—it *did* hurt. Rather liked it, though. Wish you had another sandwich. O-o-o-oh, I'm getting giddy! [*She giggles. She tucks her skirt between her legs.*] You *will* respect me, won't you? On the way down.

Almanstar. But, Miss Almenside, I respect you *already.*

Almenside. Oh, don't be naughty. You *know* what I mean. [*She giggles and flops her arm onto his shoulder.*] O-o-o-o-oh my, I really *am* getting giddy.

Almanstar. Miss Almenside, let's leave the Tour! We

can go on to Hawaii by ourselves. We don't *need* American Express!

Stunned pause.

Almenside. Leave the Tour?

Almanstar. Why not?

Almenside. Mr. Almanstar: I am perched here on the top of some very tall mountain, I'll probably be late for dinner, I have mail waiting for me in Katmandu. And yet *you're* asking me to *leave the Tour?*

Almanstar. That's right. [*She laughs contemptuously.*] . . . Well?

Almenside. Well, one just doesn't *do* such things. I think we'd better start back now.

Almanstar. Have your mail forwarded.

Almenside. What about my dinner?

Almanstar. We'll make it in time.

Almenside. Ho-ho-ho! It took us *five hours* getting up!

Almanstar. It's always faster going down.

Almenside. Well, what about our deposits?

Almanstar. I'm sure they'll refund what's left.

Almenside. They weren't very pleasant, you know, when I told them where we were planning to spend the day.

Almanstar. Well . . . they're stuffy.

Almenside. They really *are* stuffy! We got to Karachi, on the Arabian Sea? Well, it was so blessed hot! Anyway, it seems there were some *sharks* in the water. . . . [*She laughs.*] Well, I happen to be a very fast swimmer. I can handle myself! But would American Express hear of it? No. They shut me in the bus and locked the door! Well. I am *tired,* Mr. Almanstar, of being treated in this world like a helpless child. Having to take care of five-year-old kids all the time is bad enough.

Almanstar. Are you a schoolteacher, too?

Almenside. First grade. Trenton, New Jersey. Hey!

Almanstar. What?

Almenside. Ever done any surfboarding?

Almenstar. No. Why?

Almenside. Well, if we *did* go to Hawaii, that's what

I'd like to try. I've never done it either. Hear it's tough as hell.

Almanstar. Well, you know my philosophy: if the body's tough, and the mind is tough, there's *nothing* a man can't do.

ALMENSIDE *stares at him in awe. Long pause.*

Almenside. Here. Let me take your picture. [*She snaps his picture.*] Now. You take one of me. [*She hands him the camera.*] This way, you see, when we're old and gray and have had dozens and dozens of children, we'll be able to take out the family album and remember how we met. Whoops! Shouldn't have said that, maybe. Oh, well. [*She giggles, stands up.*] Hello, World! [*She falls off the peak and disappears into the cloud.*]

Almanstar [*peering over*]. Miss Almenside?

She climbs back up, a trifle dazed.

Almenside [*waving her purse in the air*]. Found it!

ALMANSTAR *snaps her picture.*

Almanstar. Well. Guess we'd better start heading back.

Almenside. Mr. Almanstar?

Almanstar. Yes.

Almenside. Here. [*She digs into her purse. She pulls out a tiny penlight.*] In case it gets too dark.

ALMANSTAR *smiles at her. He motions toward her skirt.*

Almanstar. I'll lead the way.

Almenside. Oh. [*She blushes.*] It doesn't matter any more.

And so they descend into the cloud, hand in hand, the penlight lighting the way. A short pause. The ladder reappears, THE CHINESE SOLDIER *clinging to it. He takes off his oxygen mask.*

The Chinese Soldier.
Confucius say, "Great climb can be sustained
More easily if ladder first obtained."
So, ladder set, up Everest I climbed:
A most ingenious trip—and most ill-timed.
For at the top I found I'd been preceded

By people for whom oxygen not needed.
In brief it now appears: to climb this slope
One has no need of shoes, gloves, guides, or rope.
One needs, in fact, no special mountain schooling.
One only needs not know what one is doing.
For that's how *they* accomplished it—the fools!
Came up, went down, and disobeyed the rules.
What rules?
I cheated; they outcheated me,
And all of China's best technology.
They conquered for they knew not what they fought.
(As love is only found when love's not sought.)
And so this fabricated tale is ended:
Inconsequential; and, I fear, unmended.
Therefore, I will descend and from you hide;
Along with Almanstar and Almenside.

The ladder descends into the cloud. He descends with it.

Curtain.

THE DAY THE WHORES CAME OUT TO PLAY TENNIS

TO PLAY TENNIS

A Play in One Act

CHARACTERS

FRANKLIN DELANO KUVL, *President of the Cherry Valley Country Club, aged forty-seven*

HERBERT HOOVER KUVL, *his son, Chairman of the Junior Membership Committee, aged twenty-five*

MAX (OLD GAYVE), *Secretary of the Cherry Valley Country Club, aged seventy-four*

RUDOLPH (WOLF), *his son, Chairman of the Sports Committee, aged thirty-three*

ALEXANDER RATSCIN, *Treasurer of the Cherry Valley Country Club, aged fifty-nine*

DUNCAN, *an English valet*

Various Female Voices

SCENE—The entire action takes place at the Cherry Valley Country Club.

THE DAY THE WHORES CAME OUT
TO PLAY TENNIS

A room, which has always been called the Nursery. Dawn. Sun rises during the scene. May—the tennis nets are up, but it is cold on the courts with the frost of early morning. The bay windows at the rear, which overlook the courts, are closed.

KUVL *is sitting at a children's play table, a telephone cradled in his right shoulder. He wears an overcoat, the collar turned up. His fingers tap nervously on the table. At another tiny table, engaged in a game of cards, sit* OLD GAYVE *and* ALEXANDER RATSCIN. OLD GAYVE *wears pajamas, an oversized, buttoned-wrong sweater, a wool cap, and a large, shaggy scarf.* RATSCIN *wears full-dress tuxedo except for the shirt, which is a pajama top. The lapels of his tuxedo are turned in in an attempt to hide this fact.* HERBERT, KUVL's *son, sits on a hobbyhorse, reading. He is in tuxedo and rather disheveled. Near the horse is a huge and glorious castle, somewhat in the style of Gaudi, made entirely of children's blocks.*

OLD GAYVE. I remember once, years ago, my son was very small, very young, maybe four or five, and his mother, may she rest in peace, brought him here to this room, which we're in—brought him here to play. And amongst the other children playing was this one little girl playing by herself in a crib. Well, his mother, may she rest in peace, left him with the others and went away. *When she came back!* . . . his head and shoulders were stuck between the bars of the crib. They had to saw the bars off to get him free. We never figured out just why it was he got himself into this strange predicament. But in any case he was very upset by it and his mother never brought him here again.

Ratscin. Throw a card.

Old Gayve. I think that's a funny story.

Ratscin. Knowing your son, he was probably trying to rape the girl. Now throw a card. [*Silence.*] Max.

Old Gayve. That is the only time I was ever in this room. Yes. Before today, the *only time.* Funny . . . It was May also, like now.

RATSCIN *sighs and turns to* KUVL.

Ratscin. Any news yet?
Kuvl. I'll tell you when.
Ratscin. Throw a card!

OLD GAYVE *throws a card.*

Old Gayve. I came, you see, because he was in trouble. He was my only son, and I came because he was in trouble. Yes, even then I was a silly, old man.

Ratscin. Psst! *Max.* [*This snaps* OLD GAYVE *out of his dream. He grins and reaches into his pocket, then draws out his hand and extends it.* RATSCIN *goes through the ritual of shaking his hand. An electric buzzer goes off.* RATSCIN *pulls his hand away, not, one might say, overly surprised.* OLD GAYVE *is convulsed with laughter. He throws a card.*] You've thrown two cards.

OLD GAYVE *stops laughing.*

Old Gayve. I'm sorry. [*He reshuffles the deck.*]
Kuvl. Ah, now we're getting somewhere. Yes. Right. What?
Herbert. Here, listen to *this* great line! Jake Barnes—who's the hero of the book—has just met this beautiful——
Kuvl. Ssh!
Ratscin. Yeah. *Ssh!* You've caused enough trouble for one day.
Kuvl. Hm-hm. Well, listen. You just tell her to get her ass down here on the phone, huh. . . . Because a catastrophe has occurred, *that's* why. Hm? *Catastrophe* . . . No, I will *not* spell it! [*He puts his hand over the receiver.*] She's crying.
Old Gayve. Well, a decent person doesn't speak to a five-year-old girl like *that.*
Kuvl. She was six in November. Meloney!? *Shut up and listen to your father.* [*Short pause. Then he winks to the others. Obviously, she's become quiet.*] All right, now. Tell

that woman upstairs that I wish to speak to her on the phone. . . . *What woman?* The ugly one. . . . Oh, you mean only Mommy's upstairs? Well, then . . . [*He grins.*] I guess she'll have to do.

HERBERT *slams his book shut.*

Herbert. Look, I don't think——

Kuvl. You are twenty-five years old, Herbert. It's high time you realized, your mother is *ugly!*

Old Gayve [*dealing the cards*]. Tsk-tsk-tsk-tsk-tsk-tsk——

Kuvl. Yes, Meloney. What? You called upstairs . . . and your mommy said *what?* "She'd be on the phone . . . as soon as she brushed her teeth." . . . Uh, yes, Meloney. That'll be all. [*To* HERBERT.] *Your mother!* . . . is the only woman I have ever met who will not talk to anyone on the phone in the morning, even her husband, until she has brushed her goddamned *teeth!* Now mind you, in Spain, I have known her to go without wiping her ass. But brushing her *teeth?* Never!

Old Gayve [*to* RATSCIN, *sotto voce*]. He shouts all the time.

Kuvl. Well, someday I'm going to take this hand, you see this hand? Well, someday I'm going to take it and right in the middle of her tobacco-stained teeth I am going to gently but firmly mash it, and *twist* it, and *push* it, and *shove* it! I need a drink. Get the butler, what's his name, Diggary, Deacon, Dedkin, Duncan. Oh, God. This day will be the——

KUVL *grabs his head in despair as* HERBERT *exits. Short pause.*

Old Gayve [*laughing*]. How cold it is for May. My hands are numb. [*He rubs them together.*] I will tell you something, Ratscin. And I hope you're not offended. But the trouble with you is you've had no children. Your life's been wasted, that's what. [*He laughs.*]

Ratscin. Throw a card.

Old Gayve. Were you offended?

Ratscin. Just throw a card.

OLD GAYVE *throws. The game proceeds.*

Old Gayve [*distantly, almost to himself*]. Yes, I re-member this place so well. My son kissed me, you know, when I walked into the room. Yes. That's true. He kissed me.

A *pause.*

Kuvl. Ah, at last. The breath of spring itself. Morning, Sylvia. Look, hold on a second, will you? [OLD GAYVE *has started crying. To* RATSCIN.] What the hell's wrong with *him?*

Ratscin. I donno. He just started crying.

Kuvl. Well, get him to *keep quiet, huh!?*

Ratscin. Pssst, *Max.* Keep quiet.

OLD GAYVE *looks up, stops crying, smiles, reaches into his pocket, draws out his hand, shakes hands with* RATSCIN. *An electric buzzer goes off.* OLD GAYVE *laughs.* RATSCIN *looks at* KUVL. *He shrugs.* KUVL *nods with dismal understanding.*

Old Gayve. Come, the game continues!

OLD GAYVE *throws. They resume play.* KUVL *calms down before talking.*

Kuvl. Hello. You still there? Good. Listen. I was telling some of the fellas before that *you* were the breath of spring, and, uh, *they* would like to know what kind of toothpaste you use to achieve this. No, of course I'm not joking. The fellas would like to know what kind of—— Hm? [*To the others.*] *Rum.* . . . Well. That answers that. [*Into the phone.*] That's a, uh, bit strong for the morning, isn't it, uh, dear? . . . Ah. [*To the others.*] She says the chlorophyll counteracts the rum. [*Into the phone.*] That's nice. [*To the others.*] The doctor takes her off booze, so she gets on toothpaste. [*Into the phone.*] Listen darling, the reason I called is I'd like you to do me a favor. . . . What? . . . Yes, dear, that's right! Seven o'clock in the morning—*not* a good hour for doing favors. Hm? [*Enter* DUNCAN, *in tie and tails. He is followed almost immediately by* HERBERT.] Well, because it's *important,* that's why! Because a *catastrophe* has just occurred! [*To* RATSCIN.] *She's* crying now.

Ratscin. Gin.

Old Gayve. All I do is lose money here.

Kuvl [*spotting* Duncan]. Ah, there you are. Thank God. Scotch 'n' soda. [*To the others.*] Anyone?

Old Gayve. A cup of tea. A little lemon.

Ratscin *shakes his head.*

Herbert. Orange juice, maybe, and an English muffin. [Duncan *starts to exit.*] And *tear* it, don't *cut* it!

Exit Duncan, *with a slight glance almost back.* Kuvl *puts the phone back to his ear.*

Kuvl [*to the others*]. Still going strong. Fantastic. [*Into the phone.*] Sylvia, listen to me. I have a plan. . . . Sylvia, shut up with your crying for a second and listen to me, will you, I have a *plan!* Good. Here's the plan. If *you* do this one little favor for *Daddy,* then *someday Daddy* will have to do a little favor for *you.* Now. How's *that* for a plan? [*To the others.*] One thing about Sylvia, she never turns down a deal. Even if it's lousy. [*Into the phone.*] Ah, you're an angel. Now. Run next door and . . . What? [*To the others.*] She's not wearing any clothes. [*Into the phone.*] Well, listen, my love, don't worry. No one will look at you. . . . Hm? . . . No. *No!* I don't mean *that.* Of—of *course* people would look. People are *dying* to look . . . at you, Sylvia. I mean . . . people come up to me all the time and say, "Boy! I can just imagine what your wife must look like without any clothes on." [*He chuckles. Stops.*] What do you mean, "What does that mean?" It means—— [*Short pause.*] Your body is a *mystery,* Sylvia. . . . Yes, of course that's a compliment. Why did I say then that no one would look? Uh . . . because . . . everyone would still be asleep! [*He grins proudly at his friends.*] What? Fine. [*To the others.*] She's gonna put a coat on. *Just in case.* [*Into the phone.*] Hm? No, it's *not* too late in the year for mink. [*To the others.*] She's giggling. Thinks the idea of being naked under a mink coat is *sexy.* Oh, God, what did I ever do? [*Into the phone.*] Ah, splendid. All covered up. [*To the others.*] Decency returns to Cedarville. [*Into the phone.*] Now.

Here's what I'd like you to do. I'd like you to run next door, wake up that bastard Rudolph and tell him to get the hell over here. His phone's off the hook. . . . The Club! Yes, I'm *at the Club.* . . . *Sylvia!* Tell him we'll be waiting *in the Nursery.* [*He hangs up.*] Wonderful thing about Sylvia. Anyone else would say, "What the hell're you doing in the Nursery?" Sylvia? No. All she's wondering is: will Rudolph, after all these years, finally rape her. [*Pause.*] Oh, God, how I wish he would.

Old Gayve. I don't know why I play cards with you. Here it is, seven o'clock in the morning, and already I've lost five hundred dollars.

Ratscin. You play for the pleasure.

Old Gayve. For the pleasure of playing with *you,* Ratscin. Not someone else. I like playing with *you.*

Ratscin. We've played for many years, Max.

Old Gayve. And if it costs me money, what does that matter?

Ratscin. We've played for many years.

Old Gayve. What?

Ratscin. For many years, Max. We've been playing for many years.

Old Gayve. I like playing cards with *you,* Ratscin. That's why.

Kuvl. Old Gayve, tell me. Did my father used to play with you?

Old Gayve. Yes. He beat me too. Everyone beats me. I don't know how to play cards. I'm just a silly, old man. Luckily I have enough money. Hm?

Kuvl. I wish I could have seen those games.

Old Gayve. You never saw?

Kuvl. I . . . don't remember. That's funny, isn't it? I was here.

Ratscin. I remember.

Old Gayve. We *all* used to play, right? Every night, without fail. *Every night* . . . without fail.

Ratscin. Your father and I took turns beating Old Gayve.

Old Gayve. And I never minded. Even then, I liked who

I was playing with. Maybe I should have learned how to play. As it is, I just pick cards and throw cards. I will admit it. I *don't* know what I'm doing.

Ratscin. Throw.

Old Gayve. But then you see, if I *did* . . . maybe people wouldn't like so much to play with Old Gayve.

Ratscin. That's not true.

Old Gayve. I know. My throw. [*He throws.*]

Ratscin. Gin.

Old Gayve. You see? I'll lose two thousand dollars today. Watch. [*He laughs and slaps* RATSCIN *warmly on the shoulder.*]

               Enter DUNCAN *with tray.*

Herbert. I said *orange* juice, not grapefruit!

Duncan. Yes, sir. This *is* orange.

Kuvl. Here. I'll sign.

Herbert. It *looks* like grapefruit.

Duncan. But *tastes* like orange. [*He gives* KUVL *the check to sign.*] Thank you, sir.

Herbert. Why doesn't it *look* like orange if it's orange?

Duncan. I work *inside*, sir. I don't pick the crop.

Kuvl. Herbert, keep quiet will you?

Old Gayve [*to* RATSCIN, *sotto voce*]. Always, with the help, he gets like this. Why?

               DUNCAN *hands* OLD GAYVE *his tea.*

Ratscin [*pulling his jacket closed*]. I wish I had a proper shirt on.

Old Gayve. Thank you, Duncan.

Herbert [*tasting the juice*]. I think this is orange-and-grapefruit *mix*.

Duncan. Well, perhaps, sir, you'd like to bring your *own* fruits with you next time. [*He smiles politely and starts to leave.*]

Herbert. I just may *do* that!

Duncan. Do that, sir. I'd *love* to *squeeze* them. [*Exit* DUNCAN, *with a grin.*]

Herbert. Goddamned faggot.

Ratscin. Well? Should we play another hand?

Old Gayve. Always, with the help, he's like that. It's not nice.

Ratscin. I'll deal.

Herbert. Father?

Kuvl [*who has gone to the window and is staring out*]. What?

HERBERT *goes over to his father and whispers to him.*

Old Gayve. Ah, a new hand. Maybe I'll win. [*He reaches into his pocket and takes out a cigar.*] Here. Have one of these.

Kuvl. What?

Herbert. Well, he's a faggot.

Kuvl. And *that's* why you want him fired?

Herbert. I don't like the idea of faggots working in our *kitchen!*

The cigar that OLD GAYVE *had given to* RATSCIN *explodes on being lit.*

Old Gayve [*laughing*]. It was made in Havana.

Herbert [*who had started back to his hobbyhorse, but now stops*]. I don't like the idea of them putting their hands all over my *foooood!* My *wife's* food! My *children's foooood!*

Kuvl. Sit down and shut up.

Old Gayve. I'm losing two thousand dollars and he's screaming about food.

Herbert. It's not the food, it's the *principle!*

Ratscin. Look, you've caused enough problems for one day!

Kuvl [*to himself*]. Idiot.

Herbert. I'm sorry about that . . . Mr. Ratscin.

Old Gayve [*bringing forth a chocolate bar*]. Here. Have a chocolate bar. [HERBERT *shakes his head and walks past. To* RATSCIN.] Look what happens. You open it . . . [*He opens the wrapper. A paper butterfly is sprung out.*] Nice, huh?

Ratscin [*to* KUVL]. I wish, when you called, you'd told me we'd have this much time. I'd have found a proper shirt somewhere. Florence, you see, threw my *tuxedo* shirt into the hamper as soon as we got home. I don't wear a shirt more than once. It isn't right. Wearing a wrinkled shirt is *rude*. Well, no sooner was my shirt in the hamper than you called, telling me to come back. Now of course everyone here will say, "In such a case you should have put on another *type* of shirt." But I'm afraid that isn't true. One must only wear a *tuxedo* shirt with a tuxedo. And certainly never a wrinkled one. [*He laughs at this thought.*] So. I put on a pajama top. You see? . . . [*He opens his jacket.*] Under here . . . a pajama top. *That* way, if some passer-by saw me, he'd know something was wrong—an emergency— "Look at Alexander Ratscin! He had to get dressed in a hurry," he'd say . . . and wouldn't think I simply had no taste in clothes. [*He smiles triumphantly and checks through his hand.*]

Herbert. But Mr. Ratscin, why didn't you simply take off your tuxedo and put on a suit? Then you could have worn *any* kind of shirt.

RATSCIN *stares at him in horror.*

Kuvl. I'll bet Sylvia's gone gack to bed.

Old Gayve. Rudie gets up, I think, around ten. We *could* always send a telegram, if you——

Kuvl. Why the hell does that idiot have to keep his phone off the hook? Hunh? *Tell me that!*

Old Gayve [*calmly*]. Rudie is not an idiot. [*To* RATSCIN.] Well, are you playing or dreaming?

Ratscin. He's right, you know.

Old Gayve. What?

Ratscin. I *could* have changed into a suit.

Kuvl. I suppose he wants to sleep "undisturbed," hm? I suppose he's afraid someone's gonna *call* him!

Old Gayve. Look, I'm playing cards. Don't bother me. [*To* RATSCIN.] Pick up your hand, will you?

Kuvl. Does he *usually* get phone calls at seven o'clock in the morning?

Old Gayve. Look, what do you think I am, a wire tapper? I'm an old man. Leave me alone. Your father never would have talked this way.

Kuvl. My *father* never *talked.*

Old Gayve. Maybe *that's* why *he* was a *good* president.

Kuvl. Maybe he was a good president because he didn't have so many *idiots* around.

Herbert. Hey! Listen to *this* great line. Lady Brett Ashley has just——

Kuvl. Oh, *shut up,* already! You've been reading that same book now for *five lousy weeks.*

Herbert. I don't think it's nice to make fun of someone who has a reading problem.

Old Gayve [*sotto voce*]. Talking about idiots.

Ratscin. Indeed . . . not only *could* I have changed . . . as it turns out, I *should* have.

Old Gayve. What?

Ratscin. Kuvl!

Kuvl. Hm.

Ratscin. Gimme your overcoat, quick!

Kuvl. What?

Ratscin. Look, don't ask questions, just lemme have your overcoat!

Kuvl. It's *cold.*

Ratscin. It's *not* cold.

Kuvl. What're you, out of your mind?

Ratscin. Wha' d'you mean?

Kuvl. Who the hell needs an overcoat if it isn't cold?

Ratscin. I do.

Kuvl. Fine. I need it more.

Ratscin. Look. There's still a chance Duncan hasn't seen what I'm wearing!

Kuvl. So. What're you wearing? . . . Hm. A *tuxedo and a pajama top.* Well-l-l . . .

Ratscin. What?

Kuvl. You're right. It's not such a good combination.

Ratscin. It's *not* the combination! It's the *tuxedo!* I shouldn't be wearing it at *all!*

Kuvl. Why? Isn't it yours?

Ratscin. Of *course* it's *mine!* You moron.

Kuvl. Well then, why the hell do you—— Get *away* from *me!* Why do you want my overcoat then?

Ratscin. Because *one shouldn't wear tuxedo during the day.* There.

Kuvl. Hunh?

Ratscin. In hurrying to get over here I made a silly mistake. I kept on my tuxedo when I should have changed into a suit. . . . *Well,* it may not seem like much to you. But to *me* it *matters!* I don't want Duncan to notice. I don't want to become the laughingstock of the help.

Herbert. *I'm* still wearing *my* tuxedo.

Ratscin. You're the laughingstock *already.*

Herbert. Mr. Ratscin!

Old Gayve. Not only that! You're the cause of all our *troubles, too.*

Herbert. Mr. *Gayve!*

Old Gayve. Well, my Rudolph is going to come and solve everything. You watch.

Ratscin. All right, now gimme your coat!

Kuvl. Hey, get away! Stop! *Stop!* [RATSCIN *pulls open* KUVL's *overcoat.* KUVL *is in* B.V.D.'s. *Stunned pause.*] Well, what the hell did you think *I* was wearing?

Enter DUNCAN.

Duncan. Whoops, sorry! [KUVL *pulls his overcoat closed.* RATSCIN *jumps behind him.*] Didn't know I was interrupting something. [*He turns to leave.*]

Ratscin. Duncan!

Duncan. Sir?

Ratscin. I want no laughter around here.

Duncan. Laughter?

RATSCIN *takes a deep breath and steps forward.*

Ratscin. I suppose you're wondering why it is I'm wearing a tuxedo—since, as we both well know, tuxedo is not usually worn during the day. *Well,* the answer is: my brother Harold has just died. His funeral is this afternoon. And I am going to his funeral.

Duncan. Yes, sir. As indeed you should.

Ratscin. Anyway, tuxedos are allowed at funerals. And *that's* why I want no laughter.

Duncan. I see your point.

Ratscin. You'll tell the others?

Duncan. Yes, sir. Laughter will cease at once.

Ratscin. Good. This is to be a day of mourning for us all.

Duncan. And if I may say so, sir, a welcome relief *that* will be.

Ratscin. Hm?

Duncan. I mean, how welcome it will be not to hear any laughter. If you ask me, sir, you've been a little too lax with the help. On that matter. Laughter . . . I don't know if you've noticed, but it's gotten so they're practically laughing all the time. While they mix the drinks, while they manicure the putting greens. While they scrub the dance floor. While they clean out the pool. I think, sir, a day of mourning may be just what the doctor ordered. [*He chuckles.*] If you see what I mean.

Ratscin. I'm . . . not so sure.

Duncan. One thing, however.

Ratscin. Yes?

Duncan. Just a very *minor* thing. Probably none of my business.

Ratscin. Yes?

Duncan. But don't you think the occasion calls for a somewhat less—um—*noisy* shirt?

Ratscin. This is *not* a shirt! This is a pajama top!

Duncan. Ah, yes, well, you know . . . sir. [*He clears his throat nervously.*] That sort of thing usually doesn't go over very well at funerals, either. . . . I'll send Mr. Rudolph in. [*Exit.*

RATSCIN *is staggered, to say the least.*

Kuvl. Does he mean to say that *all this time*, Rudolph has been waiting outside! [*To* RATSCIN.] You numbskull.

Enter RUDOLPH, *dressed "sharply": loud sport jacket, open collar with ascot, sunglasses.*

Rudolph. All right, so what the hell're you doing in the Nursery?

Kuvl. Sit down.

Herbert [*with awe*]. Hello, Wolf.

Rudolph [*to* KUVL]. Wait'll you hear about your wife!
You'll die laughing. [*He sits.*] I was lying in bed with this
chick, see, when Sylvia comes barging into the room, all
dolled up in mink.

Kuvl. No, on second thought. Stand up. Come over here.

Rudolph. I haven't gotten to the funny part, yet.

Kuvl. Just come over.

Rudolph. Wha'd I, say something wrong? [*He rises
wearily, petting* HERBERT's *hobbyhorse as he passes.*] Nice
horse you got there.

Herbert. Thanks, podner.

Rudolph. Dumb shit.

Old Gayve. Rudie!

Rudolph [*to* OLD GAYVE]. And *you* stay out of this! If
I'd known you were here, I wouldn't of come. All right,
what gives? [KUVL *motions with his head toward the window.* RUDOLPH *looks out. He rushes to the windowpane.
He stares out. After a few moments he turns back to the
others.*] Cra-a-zy.

Ratscin. They arrived about six thirty.

Kuvl. All eighteen of 'em.

Old Gayve. We counted.

Herbert. I was the first to see them. I was sleeping on
the couch by the front door. There'd been this party, you
see, and——

Rudolph. I *know* about the party, thank you.

Herbert. Oh, *that's* right, you were—well, anyway, I
was——

Old Gayve. He was *drunk! Dead drunk.*

Herbert. I *wasn't* drunk! I was *tired.*

Ratscin. What *I* wanna know is, if you were so tired,
how come you didn't go *home* to sleep? You think it
looks *nice*, someone sleeping on the front couch? The front
couch is for *sitting.*

Old Gayve. Right.

Ratscin. Not for sleeping.

Rudolph. Oh look, come *on*, will you?

Ratscin. Guests come into the Club. They see the *son* of our *president* sleeping on the front couch! Do you think that gives a nice impression?

Rudolph. You know what, Alex? I couldn't care less. All I wanna know is, how come there are eighteen women standing out there on our tennis courts looking like the wrath of God?

Pause.

Herbert [*calmly pompous*]. If I feel like sleeping on the front couch, *no* one can tell *me* to——

Kuvl. Herbert! Be a nice boy. Tell the man what happened. Before I knock you on the ground.

Rudolph. Might not be a bad idea anyway.

Kuvl. And *you* keep your nose *out* of it! I'm in no mood today for *your* lousy tricks!

Old Gayve. *You* can't talk to my son in that tone of——

Rudolph. Oh, *shut up!* Old fool.

Ratscin. I don't think it's proper for a son to talk to his father like——

Kuvl. Alex!

Ratscin. Sorry.

Kuvl. All right, Herbert; proceed with the story. I need an aspirin. Who's got an aspirin? This day'll be the death of me yet.

The door opens. DUNCAN *peers in.*

Duncan. One aspirin, coming up! [*He flips an aspirin tablet into the room.*]

Herbert. You think he's been listening at the keyhole?

Rudolph. No, he's just efficient. Go on with the story.

Kuvl. Someone get me that aspirin first.

HERBERT *goes in search of the pill.*

Ratscin. Do you think it's right, Frank, to take an aspirin tablet that's just been on the floor?

Kuvl. With my headache, Alex, I'd take an aspirin tablet that had just been in a shit can!

The door opens. Enter DUNCAN.

Duncan. All out of shit cans at the moment, sir. Sorry.
[*Exit.*

Herbert. I think I just stepped on the aspirin.

Rudolph. That's called "granulated." You want it? I'll scoop it up.

Kuvl. Forget it. Go on with the story. I don't believe this whole thing. [*He lets his head collapse onto the table. He covers his head with his hands.*]

Herbert. Well! Anyway! There I was. Sleeping on the couch. The one near the front door? When suddenly, I woke up. It was bright out. The place was empty. I remember thinking to myself, *something's wrong.* I guess that's what you call a "premonition." [*He giggles.*]

Kuvl. Tell 'em about the cars, Herbie.

Herbert. Um, the cars. Well. There were these two *cars,* see. Just sort of . . . sitting in the front driveway? I noticed them 'bout five minutes after I woke up. . . . I've no idea how long they'd been waiting.

Kuvl. Describe them.

Herbert. They were Rolls Royces.

And then HERBERT *starts to giggle.* RUDOLPH *stares, dumb-founded.*

Rudolph. All right. I'll buy. What's funny about two Rolls Royces?

Herbert. They were all painted over.

Kuvl. Like old jalopies.

Herbert. You know. Things like: "Put it here, baby," "Up the Ol' Missouri," "Doris Loves Dick."

Ratscin. Well. I ask you, my friend, imagine, if you can, what will happen when the Rolls Royce company hears of that! Ahhh, now *there's* a scene.

Herbert. They had raccoon tails on the aerials, as well.

Ratscin. No, no question. The worst *possible* taste. [*He taps on the table for emphasis.*]

Kuvl. Alex.

Ratscin. What?

Kuvl. Shut up!

Old Gayve [*to* RATSCIN, *sotto voce*]. Want a chocolate bar?

OLD GAYVE *cracks open the chocolate bar. A paper butter-fly springs loose.* KUVL *glares at him, finally calms down.*

Kuvl. O.K., Herbie. *Continue.*

Herbert. Well, soon as I spotted them I went outside and walked over, tried to look in, you know?—see who the passengers were, see who was driving? I mean it's not *every day* that a person comes across a pair of jalopies as expensive as *that!* [*He laughs.*]

Kuvl. Herbie.

Herbert. Well—anyway—there I was. Peering in. But—— [*He shrugs.*] No use. The sun was hitting the windows in such a way, you see, that no matter how I looked, all I could see was my reflection. . . .

Silence.

Rudolph [*when he realizes that* HERBERT *for some reason is not going on*]. Well, all right—all *right*—what happened then?

Silence.

Kuvl. Herbert. Finish the story.

Herbert. I'm sorry, but this isn't orange juice. I don't know what it is—grapefruit, orange-and-grapefruit mix, Hawaiian Punch, it doesn't matter. It isn't orange. He was *lying.*

Kuvl. Herbert?

Herbert. Do you understand what I said? He was *lying.* I want him *fired!* I want him out of here. Today. We must get him out of here today! It is *imperative* that we get him out of here *today!*

Stunned pause.

Rudolph [*sotto voce*]. Pssst . . . Frank. [*He draws* KUVL *aside.*] There's a doctor I know in——

Kuvl [*turning from him sharply*]. Hey! Herbert.

Herbert. Hm?

Kuvl. Fool everyone. Pretend you're a well-balanced person. Finish the story.

Herbert. I'm sorry.

Kuvl. Don't mention it. Just *finish* the *story.*

Herbert. I don't know what came over me. I suddenly just——

Kuvl. Yeah. Fine. *Finish* your *story!*

Herbert. I forgot where I was.

KUVL *bangs his head with his hand.* RUDOLPH *stifles a laugh.*

Ratscin. You'd just tried to see in through the car windows and couldn't.

Herbert. Oh, yeah. Right. The two-way mirror thing. Right. . . . Well, I went back to the clubhouse figuring I'd just, you know, sit on the steps and wait? Anyhow, it seems the cars were parked directly in front of the Club. So, when *I* sat down in front of the Club and looked at *them,* what I saw in the windows was *myself,* sitting in front of the Club, looking at *me.* Well. This, of course, was quite fascinating. Especially when you realize that whoever was in those cars was probably *also* looking at me. I remember thinking: I hope my fly is zipped.

Kuvl. Herbert. . . .

Herbert. You see. They weren't simply mirrors. The windows on their cars were two-way mirrors. [*He laughs slightly. Stops laughing. Short pause.*] Well. Sometime later a cloud, I guess, drifted off 'cause the sunlight started growing stronger. In fact, after a while it grew so strong that the glare of the reflection became terrible, and I had to shut my eyes. [*A pause.*] That's when they got out.

Rudolph. When your eyes were shut.

Herbert. That's right.

Rudolph. So in other words you didn't actually *see* them getting out.

Herbert. No.

Kuvl. What the hell're you driving at, Rudolph? Are you doubting my son's word?

Rudolph. Oh. No. I'm just curious how one goes about fitting eighteen women into two cars. Twenty, if you include the drivers.

Ratscin. Maybe two of the *women* were driving. Oh, I will admit a Rolls Royce is not usually seen without a chauffeur. But then, a Rolls Royce is not usually seen with raccoon tails waving from the aerials either. No. In a case like this, my friend, *anything* is possible.

Rudolph. Except that the cars aren't there any longer.

So someone must have driven them off.

Kuvl. They're not there?

Old Gayve. They were there when *I* arrived.

Ratscin. Me, too.

Rudolph. All right, forget it! The *chauffeur* drove them off, and most of the women rode in the trunk. They're an escaped vaudeville act. Go on with the story.

Herbert [*to* KUVL]. Maybe I should describe what they were wearing.

Kuvl. Good.

Herbert [*to* RUDOLPH, *merrily*]. I'm gonna describe what they were wearing!

Rudolph. Why? Weren't they wearing what they're wearing now?

Herbert. Oh, no! When I first saw them they were *elegant.* The most elegant women I'd ever seen. They wore long black satin dresses that swept the ground when they walked. And all over their dresses were diamonds as large as eggs. In their hair were egret feathers. And on their shoulders, chinchilla capes hanging like wings. Well, naturally I figured they were members so I let them in.

Rudolph. You let them in.

Kuvl. He let them in.

Ratscin. Just like that.

Old Gayve. What an idiot.

GAYVE *laughs.* KUVL *turns and stares at him.* GAYVE *stops laughing.*

Kuvl. Max. What my son did may not be the brightest thing. But I will not allow you to call him an *idiot!*

Rudolph. Yeah. It reflects on Frank.

Kuvl. And *you* shut up!

Ratscin [*to* KUVL, *sotto voce*]. Kuvl. Have him go on with the story, will you? I'm getting hungry sitting here.

Kuvl [*calming down*]. Go on with the story.

Herbert. Well. They all went into the clubhouse. But *I* stayed right where I was, and thought to myself, there's *something very odd about all this.* . . . Then, suddenly, sure enough, I got the answer. They were carrying *tennis* rackets! *Well-l-l-l,* women who are dressed like that just don't carry *tennis rackets.* [*He chuckles proudly.*]

Rudolph [*to* Kuvl, *sotto voce*]. He's Scotland Yard material, Frank. Scotland Yard material.

Herbert. You think I'd be good, Wolf? At Scotland Yard?

Kuvl. You'd be fantastic. Finish the story. [*To* Rudolph.] And shut up or we'll be here all day.

Ratscin. I'm getting hungry, Frank.

Kuvl. I know, I know. [*He groans and slumps forward on the table in despair.*]

Herbert. Well. Anyway. Soon as I realized this, I went in after them. Sure enough, they were out back, waiting on the courts. They'd, uh, changed into their tennis clothes. [*He tries to laugh. Can't.*] I'm afraid they weren't quite as elegant as before. For one, instead of tennis sneakers they had on basketball shoes. Instead of tennis whites they had on plaids and chartreuse and lavender. And when they bent over, it turns out they didn't have on any underpants at *all.* Well! Of course! As soon as I saw all this vulgarity I knew they weren't members. So, controlling my temper as best I could, I walked over and said, "I'm sorry, but *this* is a *private* country club. So I'm afraid you'll have to get off."

Rudolph. Hmmm. [*To* Kuvl.] He really knows how to put things well, doesn't he? Your boy . . . [*To* Herbert.] What was their response to *that* li'l gem?

Herbert. They, uh . . . started to play tennis. [*He grins idiotically.*] That's when I went inside and called up Dad.

Kuvl. I called the rest of the committee.

Ratscin. Sylvia called you.

Old Gayve. Your phone was off the hook.

Ratscin. We all came to the Nursery because it was the best place to watch.

Old Gayve. Yeah.

Herbert. So take a look at the way they play.

Kuvl. 'Cause it's probably the *strangest* part.

RUDOLPH *goes to the windows.*

Rudolph. They're good.

Ratscin. Good? They're the finest grass-court tennis players we've ever SEEN! Well. Tennis is not a game for the *hoi polloi*. It's a game for *ladies*. And *gentlemen*. Yet. There they are. The *hoi polloi*. And what are they? Better than Helen Wills.

Old Gayve. Or Alice Marble.

Ratscin. So. I ask you: *how does one figure?*

RUDOLPH *starts to laugh. A chuckle at first—it builds into a roar. Everyone stares at him dumbfounded.*

Rudolph. Oh, it's beautiful: eighteen bare-assed broads and they know how to play—it's just *beautiful*. I mean it's the greatest thing that's ever happened to the game of tennis, to say *nothing* of the goddamned Club. Oh, my God, what a fantastic day *this* is turning out to be. I mean, the place has come to *life!* [*And then he starts to laugh again, while the others continue to glare.*]

Kuvl. Um, Rudolph . . . [*He clears his throat.* RU-DOLPH *stops laughing.* KUVL *smiles in gratitude.*] It may interest you to know that the, uh, committee is of the rather unanimous opinion that this . . . *incident* . . . is not a laughing matter. Funny as it, uh, may seem.

Rudolph. What're you talking about? Oh, Frank, come off it, will you? The thing's a riot. Oh, look, just picture what's gonna happen when your *wives* catch sight of these broads. I mean *your* wives play tennis in their *girdles* for chrissake. That scene'll rock 'em to the *core*. Oh baby, look, I'm telling you, just be patient and this thing'll be a *riot*, an *absolute riot*.

Kuvl. Yes. Thank you but of, uh, *that* we're . . . already quite sure. [*He collapses onto the table again.*]

Ratscin. The *worst*, however, is the Happy Valley Country Club. Which is due here at twelve. Today being, I am sorry to report, Guest Day at our Club.

Rudolph. And you mean to say *they* won't enjoy that view?

Ratscin. Enjoy it? They'll *love* it! They'll think they're members. And that will *really* be the end of us.

Old Gayve [*to* RATSCIN, *sotto voce*]. Maybe a cigar?

RATSCIN *takes the cigar without thinking.*

Kuvl. No, Rudolph. The fact is, we must *somehow* get them off.

The cigar explodes on being lit.

Ratscin [*to* GAYVE, *not overly amused*]. Made in Havana, right?

Old Gayve [*beside himself with delight*]. Right.

HERBERT *starts to cry softly.*

Kuvl [*peering at the floor*]. Where *is* that aspirin?

KUVL *begins to stalk about, searching the floor.* RATSCIN *has relit the cigar and mashed it on* GAYVE'*s jacket.*

Old Gayve. Look! You've burned it. *Look.*

Ratscin. I'll buy you a new one.

Kuvl [*spotting the grain of aspirin*]. Ah!

Old Gayve [*weeping*]. I don't *want* a new one. I liked *this* one. My wife gave it to me just before she passed away.

Rudolph. Oh, Christ, now he's gonna start on *that* bit. We'll *never* hear the——

Kuvl. Hey! Pssst. You see this? *Aspirin.* [*He pops it into his mouth.*] But all the while I'm thinking to myself, *arsenic is what it is!* [*He pats his stomach contentedly.*]

Rudolph. Hey, this, uh, thing's really gotten to you, hasn't it? I mean—in the ol' head.

Kuvl. Yes, it's gotten to me! Of course it's gotten to me!!

Rudolph. But *why* . . . ?

Kuvl. Hm?

Rudolph. Why are you so upset? 'Cause of what the wives are gonna say? Or the Happy Valley Country Club? I'm sorry, but I just can't believe that. [HERBERT *starts crying louder.*] Oh, great. *Another* voice heard from. [*To* HERBERT.] Look, shut up, will you?

Herbert. It's all my fault. I'm the one to blame.

Rudolph. I mean I could buy reasons like that with Ratscin. Or my ol' man. 'Cause, you know, they don't know any better. Not that you know much better yourself. But at least with you, you dumb fool, there's still a little hope. [*He laughs.*]

Kuvl. Rudolph.

Rudolph [to HERBERT]. *Shut up, huh?* [*To* KUVL.] What?

Kuvl. Why do you think they're here?

Rudolph. Look, shut up already, huh? [*To* KUVL.] To play tennis. [HERBERT *sobs.*] I swear I'm gonna hit him on the head.

Kuvl. You think they came here just to play tennis.

Rudolph. I donno. Maybe they want us to screw 'em. You think we can handle nine apiece? I'm afraid we could never count on our three friends here to chip in very much help. [*He laughs.*]

Kuvl [smiling]. Well, if all else fails we could certainly go down trying.

They both laugh at this. HERBERT *wails above their laughter.*

Rudolph. Oh, shut up, will you? [KUVL *and* RUDOLPH *are still laughing.*] You know, someday I'm gonna throw him out a window. Not, mind you, because I hate him so much. But because you're a nice guy—and I'd like to do you a favor. [*To* HERBERT.] Stop *crying, will you!*

Herbert [sobbing]. It's all my fault.

Rudolph. Yeah, well fine, just keep it to yourself. [*To* KUVL.] What? You were gonna say something.

Kuvl. I was gonna say . . . it would be very nice if all that were true: that they came to play tennis—and/or make a little love. . . .

KUVL *smiles, almost laughs. But does not. A short pause.*

Rudolph. Yeah. So?

Kuvl. So? For some reason . . . I don't think that's why they came.

Rudolph. Hm?

HERBERT *sobs.* KUVL *reaches into his pocket and draws out a coin.*

Kuvl [flipping it]. Heads you kill him. Tails I kill him first. [*He looks down at the coin.*] I win. Duncan! I'll have the butler do it.

KUVL *smiles weakly, goes, sits down, holds his head in*

despair. RUDOLPH *stares at him, perplexed. Short pause. Then he turns to* HERBERT, *who is still crying. He tiptoes over to him.*

Rudolph [*whispering into* HERBERT's *ear*]. Your wife doesn't wear any underpants either.

Herbert [*bolt upright, stunned*]. What?

Rudolph. You heard me. Here we go!

RUDOLPH, *with a wild laugh, suddenly begins to rock* HERBERT *on his hobbyhorse.* HERBERT *screams and hangs on for dear life.*

Herbert. I'm gonna get sick!

RUDOLPH *roars with laughter.*

Kuvl. Rudolph!

Rudolph. Keep with it, baby. You're coming into the home stretch.

Enter DUNCAN.

Duncan. You called me, sir?

Rudolph [*patting* HERBERT *on the head*]. Good race.

Herbert. Did I win?

Rudolph. You ran the wrong way.

Kuvl. Brink me a bottle of Scotch. [*He heads for* RU-DOLPH.]

Duncan. Yes, sir. One bottle of Scotch. Coming right up.

Kuvl. O.K., now you listen to me. I've warned you just about enough. One more incident like this and, Buster, you're in for trouble.

Rudolph. Don't call me "Buster." *You* know my name.

Kuvl. I'll call you any damn thing I like.

Rudolph. Oh, *will* you?

Kuvl. Yeah! When I'm talking about my son, yeah. 'Cause, you see, I don't like the way you treat him. Now. What do you think of *that*, huh? . . . *Buster?*

Rudolph [*calmly*]. I think your son is a schmuck. [*Stunned expression on* KUVL's *face.*] Heh-heh. Gotcha, didn't it? [*To* HERBERT, *an aside.*] Teach him to pull that Edward G. Robinson crap on *me.* [*He slaps* HERBERT *on the back, walks away, smiling slightly.*]

Duncan [*to* KUVL]. Uh, begging your pardon, sir. But time certainly is a-fleeting, isn't it? [DUNCAN *winks at* KUVL *and exits.*]

KUVL *stares after him, dumbfounded by it all.*

Old Gayve [*to Ratscin*]. The thing to remember about my son is he doesn't appreciate being woken early. Sleep, you see, is his religion. And waking him too early, like today, is like disturbing a devout man in prayer—any second you should expect a plague to be on your house, and the wrath of God on your head. [GAYVE *laughs.*] Yet, you know, the strange part is, he's not a lazy boy. . . . [*A short pause. Suddenly* KUVL *rushes to the windows. He throws one open wide.*] My God! What's he doing?

The sound of tennis rackets smashing tennis balls is heard. DUNCAN *pokes his head back into the room. No one notices.*

Kuvl. Attention! Attention *please!* [*The sound dies down.*] This . . . is a *private country club!*

Rudolph. You tell 'em, Frankie boy.

KUVL *glares at* RUDOLPH.

Ratscin. Go ahead. They're listening.

Kuvl. And while we *respect* . . . [*To the others.*] This'll never work.

Ratscin. Go ahead. *Try.*

Kuvl. And while we *respect* . . . your desire to play tennis . . . we *must* request that *you* respect . . . our *rules!* [RUDOLPH *bursts out laughing.*] You know, *you're* in this boat, too!

Rudolph. Yeah. But *I* can swim, baby. Don't forget that.

Ratscin. Frank, here they come!

Herbert [*rising in his stirrups*]. What's happening?

Old Gayve. They're walking toward the clubhouse. . . . Now they've stopped.

Ratscin. What's wrong, can't you see for *yourself?*

Rudolph. He's *afraid.*

Herbert. I'm *not* afraid. . . . I just happen to be feeling sick. [*He sits back down on his hobbyhorse.*]

Old Gayve. They've all turned around. . . . Now they're bending over. They're——

Rudolph. I don't believe it.

Ratscin [stunned]. Lifting up their dresses.

Herbert. What? [*He jumps off his horse and rushes to the window.*]

A *loud indescribable noise is heard.* KUVL *slams the window closed.*

Rudolph [in total awe]. My God. That's the most amazing sound I've ever *heard.*

Ratscin. Total lack of breeding. *That's* what it shows.

Old Gayve. Doesn't smell good either.

Kuvl [picking up a telephone on the table]. Hello, hello, get me the *police!* [*He listens. He clicks the buttons up and down.*]

Herbert. What *I* want to know is, how did they do it? Eighteen women, *all at the same time.*

Old Gayve. It's like the Rockettes.

Kuvl. Hello, *police?* [KUVL, *getting no answer, pulls on the cord of the phone. At the end of the cord is another phone. Both are toys.*] Goddamned *toys!* [*He hurls the phone across the room.*] Goddamned *place!! Duncan!!!*

Ratscin [pushing over the good phone]. Here. It was on the other table.

KUVL *picks up the phone. Enter* DUNCAN, *on the run, a bottle in his hand.*

Duncan. Was that *your* voice I heard, sir? Beckoning?

KUVL *puts the receiver down on the table.*

Kuvl [to himself]. And *this* one's dead.

Duncan. I beg your pardon?

Kuvl. This *telephone* is *dead.*

Duncan. Oh. That's very sad news indeed, sir.

Kuvl. Yes it is.

Duncan. Though, if you don't mind my saying so, it *does* have its ironical side.

Kuvl. Hm?

Duncan. Well, I mean, sir, just *look* at it. There it lies, a once glorious instrument, its merry trill suddenly stilled forever. And yet, not twenty minutes ago, I stood in this very room, and that phone was *alive!* And Mr. Ratscin said to me, "Duncan . . . today shall be a day of mourning for us *all.*"

A *pause.*

Kuvl. Yes. Uh, Duncan. Get me another phone, would you? Before I hit you with this one.

Duncan. No need, sir. Your wish, as always, *my command.* [*He bows grandly and exits.*]

Ratscin. I think maybe we should find ourselves another butler.

Kuvl *suddenly rushes to the door.*

Kuvl. Duncan! Bring back that bottle of *Scotch!* [Kuvl *thrusts his arm through the open door.* Kuvl *pulls his arm back into the room, bottle in hand. He stares at the bottle.*] . . . Tequila.

The door flies open, smashing into Kuvl *as it does.*

Duncan. One telephone, just as ordered! Came as quickly as I could.

Kuvl [*rubbing his injured back*]. This is tequila.

Duncan. Whoops, sorry.   [*Exit.*

Kuvl. Leave the telephone!

Duncan's *arm reaches back in.* Kuvl *takes the new telephone from* Duncan's *hand. Exit* Duncan's *arm.*

Old Gayve. Look at that. How nervous I am. I've shuffled the two packs together.

Ratscin. Forget it. We'll play canasta.

Herbert. I think I'm gonna be sick.

Enter Duncan, *on the run, a huge sack of lemons in hand.* Kuvl *is busy jacking the phone into the wall.*

Duncan. Well! Here you are. [*He drops the sack of lemons.*]

Kuvl. What the hell is *that?*

Duncan. A sack of lemons.

Kuvl. And what the hell do I need with a sack of lemons?

Duncan. You'll find it helps the tequila.

Kuvl. I'm sure. The, uh, point, however, is that I ordered *Scotch. Not* tequila.

Duncan. Yes, sir. I know.

Kuvl. So . . . ?

Duncan. Tequila is stronger.

Kuvl *stares about, dumbfounded, dazed.*

Rudolph [*who has just tried the new phone, to* Kuvl]. This phone's out of order, too.

Kuvl. This phone's out of order, too!

Duncan. Contagious, isn't it?

Kuvl. Well, get me *another* one!

Duncan. Yes, sir! *Another* phone. Coming right up.
[*Exit.*

Kuvl *rips the phone from the wall and flings it across the room. It knocks down the castle.*

Kuvl. I think I'm gonna cry.

Old Gayve [*to* Kuvl]. You wanna play canasta? We could make it three hands.

Rudolph. Hey! There's a chick in court five who's got a better serve than Pancho Gonzalez. Now *that's* amazing.

Duncan *enters quietly.*

Kuvl. What have we done to *deserve* this? What have we done?

Duncan. I'm afraid, sir, that Miss Dorothy Duskwit, the creator of yon castle, will be most upset with you for having destroyed it. It was an authentic replica of a feudal masterpiece found still in Tarragona, Spain. And took her nearly a year to build.

Kuvl. Screw Miss Dorothy Duskwit. Plug the phone into the wall.

Duncan *goes to plug it in.* Herbert *suddenly rushes over.*

Herbert. Here, give-it-a-me! [*He grabs the phone from* Duncan.] I'll help you, Dad. [*He plugs the phone in. He listens. He looks up at* Duncan.]

Duncan. No answer, hm?

Herbert. No. No answer.

Kuvl. Whaaat!

Duncan. No answer.

Herbert. The phone's out of order.

KUVL *glares at* DUNCAN. DUNCAN *shrugs.*

Kuvl [*sudden warmth displayed*]. Duncan.

Duncan [*just as warmly*]. Yes, sir.

Kuvl. When we hired you as butler . . . what do you think we had in mind?

Duncan. Well, frankly, sir, I don't know.

Kuvl. You don't know.

The two men laugh.

Duncan. Is a teaser, isn't it?

Kuvl. Well, lemme toss *this* one out.

Duncan. See how it fits.

Kuvl. Right. . . . Has it ever occurred to you that what we wanted you for was, uh—[*he chuckles*]—*service?*

Duncan. Service?

Kuvl. Yes, you know, things like mixing drinks, waiting on tables, bringing people telephones that work. Things like that.

Duncan. You, uh, must, uh, be joking.

Kuvl. Must I?

Duncan. Without question. I mean, after all, sir, I'm just not the sort who'd *take* a job like that. [*He laughs.*] Not that I mind, of course, helping out every so often. "Lending a hand," as they say.

DUNCAN *smiles at the members. Stunned pause.*

Kuvl. Uh . . . Uh—what . . . just what do you think your . . . job *is* then?

Duncan. Well, sir, as I told you, I've never been quite sure. But, if you'll pardon me for saying this, I've always *assumed* that my job was to, um . . . help the members with their *diction.*

Kuvl. Tie him up.

HERBERT *runs the telephone cord around* DUNCAN.

Duncan. Sir, I must protest. This is no way to treat an authentic Englishman.

Kuvl. Have you got him?

Herbert. Got him.

Kuvl. All right. Now. *Why* have you brought me a phone that's *out of order!?*

Duncan. Oh, *sir*, you see *that* is the point. This phone is *not* out of order.

Kuvl. It's not.

Duncan. No, sir. It's not.

Kuvl. Well, for a phone that isn't out of order it certainly isn't working too damned *well!*

Duncan. Ah, now that's *another* matter.

Kuvl. Oh, *is* it? . . . Well, *something* is out of order in this place! And *I* wanna know what the hell it is!

Duncan. The wires.

Kuvl. Hm?

Duncan. It's the *wires* that are out of order. *Not* the phones.

Kuvl. The *wires?*

Duncan. Yes, sir. The wires. You know. Those little things that lead from the——

Kuvl. Yes, yes, I know! I *know!*

Duncan [*laughing*]. Well then, why did you——

Kuvl [*sotto voce*]. What's wrong with them?

Duncan. The wires.

Kuvl. Yes, the *wires!*

Duncan. Oh. Well, seems they've been cut.

Kuvl. CUT?

Duncan. Yes, sir. You know . . . [*He "makes like a scissor" with his fingers.* KUVL *twists the cord.*] Sir. You're *squeezing very hard.*

Kuvl. Who cut 'em?

Duncan. The ladies, sir. Under these conditions I cannot tell a lie.

A short pause. The members glance at each other uneasily.
KUVL *nods to* HERBERT. DUNCAN *is freed.*

Kuvl. All right. Here's the problem. Are you listening?

Duncan. Attentively.

Kuvl. Good. We would like very much to get in touch with the police. How do we do it?

Duncan. Now that the wires are down.

Kuvl. Now that the wires are down.

Duncan. Well, sir. I'd say what you need . . . is a wire-less. [DUNCAN *roars with laughter.* KUVL *picks up the bottle of tequila, murder in his eyes.*] Sorry, sir. Forgot the Club doesn't have one.

KUVL *glares at him. Ponders. Then puts the bottle down.*

Ratscin. Maybe we could send someone over in a car.

Kuvl. Believe me, if they bothered to cut our telephone wires, our *cars* are not going to run!

Herbert. I could *walk* over.

Kuvl. It's five miles away. [*To* DUNCAN.] So! You have no suggestions, hm?

Duncan. Not true, sir. I *have* suggestions. Just didn't know you *valued* them, that's all.

Kuvl. In times of crisis one's values quickly change.

Duncan. Yes, sir. W*ell* put.

Kuvl. L*et's hear your suggestions.*

Duncan. Right you are. [*He clears his throat.*] Well. As I see it. What *you* want is the police. The trouble is, the police don't seem to know it. And the reason for that is, to put it bluntly, you're *incommunicado.* Or, to put it another way, "cut off from the outside world." [*He chuckles.*] Well . . . [*Clears his throat.*] What you clearly need . . . is a signal.

Kuvl. A *signal.*

Duncan. A signal, yes, sir, that's right, a signal. Some sort of . . . clever signal. By which you can, as they say, "re-establish contact with the outside world."

Kuvl. Hm-hm. And just how will the, um . . .

Duncan. Outside world.

Kuvl. Yes, thank you . . : know what it means?

Duncan. Well, that's why, you see, it has to be clever. There can be no mistaking the significance of *this* signal. Anyone who notices it must be able to say to himself, "My God, but those people need *help!*" That's where the police come in. These people, you see, who notice the signal, *they'll* send the police. Unless, of course, the police have noticed it first. In which case they'll more than likely be on their way. Anyway. There are a number of signals you

can choose from. Screaming is one. Shouting "Help!" is
another. Neither of these, however, is any good since
you're too far off for anyone to hear. All that would happen I'm afraid is that you'd get very tired out. Well, what
I suggest is smoke. Good ol' reliable smoke—the "Indian
trick." Not only bring the police on the run, but the fire
department as well. And—since speed is of the essence—
you'll want the most noticeable smoke signal you can
get. Which is why I strongly recommend, sir, that you
burn down the Club. . . . *Hm,* think I'll be going.

DUNCAN *heads for the door.* RUDOLPH *catches his arm.*

Rudolph. Duncan, ol' man. I like your style. Don't go
just yet. Hm? [*He puts his arm around* DUNCAN'S *shoulder.
To the others.*] Now, come on. Leave him alone. He was
just kidding. [*To* DUNCAN.] *Weren't* you?

Duncan. Uh, yes, sir. J-just kidding. It's, uh . . . it's
my *manner.*

Rudolph. It's his manner. Kidding is his manner. So
therefore, you must leave him alone. [*To* DUNCAN.] Right?
[*Silence.* RUDOLPH *laughs and slaps* DUNCAN *on the shoulder.*] Come on. I wanna talk to you. [*He tries to take*
DUNCAN *aside.* DUNCAN *resists.*] Don't be afraid, baby. I
just wanna *talk* to you. I *like* talking to you. . . . Your
diction is so good. [*He takes* DUNCAN *aside. In a familiar
tone, friendly, confidential.*] All right. Now listen: here's
what I wanna know. Those chicks out there. You seem
kind of buddy-buddy with 'em. What's their, uh, *background?* So to speak.

DUNCAN *stares at* RUDOLPH. *Then looks at his hand on
his shoulder.*

Duncan. I'm sorry, sir. But would you mind removing
your hand?

Rudolph. Oh. 'Scuse me. [*He removes his hand.*] Well?

Duncan. Uh, don't know. Never seen the "chicks" before.

Rudolph. But you *have* talked to them. Right?

Duncan. A brief chat. At most. Yes.

Rudolph. Did you *like* 'em?

Duncan. They seemed a pleasant lot.

RUDOLPH *puts his hand back on* DUNCAN's *shoulder.*

Rudolph. They seem to go in for, uh . . . farting on the tennis courts. What d'you, uh . . . *think* of that?

Duncan. I beg your pardon?

Rudolph. I mean, do you *approve* of such behavior? Ladies [*mock British accent*] . . . farting on our tennis courts?

DUNCAN *stares about, rather befuddled.*

Duncan. I . . . don't think I quite follow what you're, uh, driving at, sir. [*He laughs weakly.*]

Rudolph. Why, then I guess I'll just have to explain it to you in, uh, *simpler English.* Hm? [*He smiles at* DUN-CAN.] Here it is. I believed, for many reasons, but mainly because of their—oh, how shall I put it?—*gastric indiscretions* [*he smiles at* DUNCAN] . . . that you'd find the ladies outside socially inferior to you. Yet—I find they're your friends. . . . This disturbs me.

Duncan. Oh, yes, now I see. [*He chuckles.*] Well, you know, sir, "To err is human; to forgive, divine." [*He laughs. Notices* RUDOLPH's *hand on his shoulder.*] Your, uh, hand if you please . . . ?

RUDOLPH *grabs* DUNCAN *by the collar of his jacket and slams him against a wall.*

Rudolph. You goddamned *sonofabitch!* Who gave you the right to make fun of my father's *diction!* That's the way he *sounds* when he talks. He can't *help* it! Do you understand what that *means? He-can't-help-it!* Well, who in hell gave you the right to make *fun* of that? I mean what do you *want?* Do you want him to sound like *you* maybe? Would *that* make him all right? If he sounded like *you?* If he had better *diction!* I mean would *that* make him . . . more *acceptable?* Hm? Well, buddy, *right here* he's *acceptable!* Right *here*, in this lousy fucking *club* he's acceptable. In fact he's better than acceptable! He's *king!* In this place he's *king! . . . My father is king!!* [*Long pause. More calmly.*] Since you're such a captive audience, I'll tell you something which maybe you didn't know. My father, the king, he cheats at cards. He's a great gin player, see. I mean he's *truly great*. He *knows* what he's *doing!* So. What does he do? He cheats. He loses on purpose so knights and prince consorts'll play with him. He pays two thousand dollars a month . . . to have *friends*. Well. Now maybe you don't like that. I mean maybe you don't *approve*. Well, maybe I don't either. But does that give you the right to come and take it all *away* from him? Take away, I mean, this—this life that he's got here, this *make-believe life* that he's got here, this little bit of *shit* that he's got here! Does that give you the right to take it all away? . . . Take away the dignity which he has found here? Which he's bought . . . which he built . . . brick by brick, fairway by fairway, putting green by *putting green!* Does *anything* give you the right to take *this all away?* I don't *think* so. 'Cause you see *I* don't think you've got anything t' offer 'm in *exchange*. I mean in simple business terms, it wouldn't be, what *we* call, a fair and equitable deal. And I just *wouldn't* wanna see my father *cheated*. He's got too large an *investment* in this place. If you follow what I mean. [*Pause. Softly.*] Now I think I'm gonna rip you apart.

He grabs DUNCAN *by the neck and is choking him when* KUVL, RATSCIN, *and* HERBERT *grab him and pull him away.* RUDOLPH, *for some reason, does not struggle very much. Instead he simply stares at* DUNCAN. DUNCAN, *massaging his neck, stands back.*

Very long pause. DUNCAN *exits from the room.*

Then through each of the windows, and in order, crashes a volley of tennis balls, breaking the glass like gunfire.

Old Gayve. I think *they're going to attack!*

The members, except RUDOLPH, *rush to the windows. They stare out. Wild sound of women's laughter from outside.*

Ratscin [*through the hole in a window*]. Attention! Attention! What you have just done is *willful destruction* of *private property!* Which is a *misdemeanor!* And *as* such, punishable by *law!* I . . . am a *lawyer!* So I *know* whereof I speak.

Slight pause before everyone leaps back from the windows. Another tennis ball per window comes crashing through. The men stare with horror at the shattered glass. Wild laughter from outside again.

Kuvl [*suddenly making for the windows*]. To the shutters!

The others dash after him. They reach through the broken windows and pull the shutters closed. They lean back and sigh. A deathly pall settles over the room. Long pause. And then the first of the tapping is heard. It is, at the start, hardly noticeable, and very infrequent. Then it is heard: a gentle tapping on the shutters. The members, when they hear, stare back in horror. At last RUDOLPH *walks over and peers through a chink in one of the shutters. He turns back.*

Rudolph [*distantly; he has seemed preoccupied during all this*]. Tennis balls. They're hitting tennis balls against the shutters.

Nervous laughter from RATSCIN *and* OLD GAYVE.

Herbert. It . . . it sounded just like . . . someone knocking. You know. . . . Asking us to let him come in? [*He giggles; stops.*]

Silence. KUVL *picks up the bottle of tequila, opens it, takes a drink.* RUDOLPH *walks away from the window and passes by* OLD GAYVE *as he does.*

Old Gayve. Thank you. For what you did before . . .

Rudolph. What?

Old Gayve. Your father thanks you for what you did for him before. . . . He appreciates it, very much.

Rudolph. You think I did that for *you?* Is *that* what you think? You think all of that was for *you?* You stupid *Jew!* You stupid, weak, Yiddish-talking patsy of a Jew! It's no *wonder* people make fun of you all the time! I make fun of you *myself! !* I mean you're a *joke!* You're no *man.* You're a *joke!* You're a stupid stupid joke! You're a sell-out, that's what! You're a sell-out as a man. And now all you are is a joke. [*Pause.*] So don't go telling people I did anything for you, you understand? I mean I'm *up* to your tricks. I mean, believe me, if I did anything I sure as hell didn't do it for you. You *understand?*

Pause.

Old Gayve. Who'd you do it for then?

Pause.

Rudolph. No one at all. [*He stares at his father.*] Which means I did it for myself. [*Then, after a moment, he turns away; walks away from him.*]

HERBERT *goes over to* RUDOLPH.

Herbert. Hey, Wolf. When you had hold of Duncan before I thought for *sure* you were gonna——

Rudolph. Fraaaaank! [*He rushes away from* HERBERT.] Your son is a *Schmuck!* Keep him away from me! He's driving me up a *wall!* [*He storms away. He paces about. After a few moments he whirls back on* KUVL.] Herbert Hoover Kuvl. How the hell could you ever name a kid Herbert Hoover Kuvl? I mean, just 'cause *your* ol' man was schmuck enough to name *you Franklin Delano* Kuvl, did you have to be a schmuck also and name your schmucky li'l kid Herbert Hoover? I mean, wha'd you, think maybe he'd follow someday in your footsteps and become, like you, a *great president* of this *illustrious country club?* Well, if you did, Frankie baby, you gave him the wrong goddamned name! . . . Boy, what an idiot you are. I mean you're a real true idiot, you know? I—I mean —I—mean, your *wife* . . . is the ideal babe for you. An idiot. With boobs down to her kneecaps. I mean you should of seen her this morning. Like she woke me up with a mink coat on—but nothing under it. Well, *hell, I* came over here only 'cause I thought if I stayed at home she might insist on going to *bed* with me. . . . Hey!— come to think of it—how the hell did you ever *get* a son? I mean don't tell me you've actually made *love* to that woman!

RUDOLPH *begins to roar with laughter.* KUVL *stares at him.*
At last the laughter fades.

Kuvl. I knew there was a reason we called you here today. You're Chairman of the Sports Committee, right?

Rudolph. Yeah. Right. What of it?

Kuvl. Just this. Seems there are some women trespassing on our tennis courts. Please get them off.

Rudolph. Hunh?

Kuvl. Well, I mean, since *you're* Chairman of the *Sports* Committee and tennis is considered a *sport,* those people out there must be *your* responsibility. Right? *Right.* So! Get them off. Will you? Like a *good* boy?

Rudolph. How the hell do you expect me to get them off?

Kuvl. I'm not Chairman of the Sports Committee.

Rudolph. I mean, what do you expect me to *reason* with 'em, tell 'em "Get off the courts," then watch 'em go?

Kuvl. I don't really know, Rudolph. It's your problem now. You've got maybe ten minutes at the most.

Rudolph. What am I supposed to do?

Kuvl. I don't *know,* Rudolph. I *told* you. I mean *you're* the *ladies'* man. *You* should know if *anyone* . . .

Long pause. The tennis balls pound against the shutters.
RUDOLPH *looks at the windows. Then he laughs.*

Rudolph. Yeah. Why not? It'll be a gas. [*He goes to the door.*] I might even bring a few of 'em back. Give li'l Herbie here a chance to tear off a piece or two. [*He laughs wildly and, hitching up his pants, winks at the committee.*] Be a little more fun out there than in *here,* anyway. That's for sure. [*He exits from the room.*]

Silence. Except for the pounding of the tennis balls.

Ratscin [*distantly, really to himself*]. My wife Florence once said she regretted our having no children. I told her, "There are other things." But secretly I checked into adoptions. For some reason, which I can't seem to remember, I decided against this. We kept on trying. My wife is attractive. Fairly attractive. So this, of course, was no chore. Anyway, nothing happened. So we went to a very fine doctor on Park Avenue to see which one of us was sterile. Not that it made much difference. But we were beginning to fight. She was saying I was sterile. I was saying *she* was sterile. Anyway, as it turns out, we *both* were sterile. The doctor said we were a perfect pair. [Ratscin *laughs*.] Today, I am successful. I am worth a quarter of a million dollars. I am known for my taste. Yet, as I was born with nothing, so, I will die with nothing. . . . No children to carry on. . . . And *yet*, sometimes I *wonder*, and I think maybe Florence wonders too: is this condition not possibly, as they say, a "blessing in disguise"? [*He turns to* Old Gayve.] Old Gayve?

Old Gayve. Hm?

Ratscin. You are my one great friend.

Pause. Old Gayve *searches in a pocket. He brings out a false nose, mustache, and eyeglasses attachment. He puts it on.*

Old Gayve. Look! Do you recognize me? [*He laughs. He slaps* Ratscin's *hand. The electric buzzer in* Gayve's *hand goes off.* Old Gayve *laughs and takes off his disguise.*] Come. I'll deal the cards.

Suddenly the pounding of the tennis balls stops.

Kuvl [*softly*]. Rudolph has been spotted. . . .

The others look up. A pause.

Herbert. Well, why doesn't anyone *look?* [*But no one moves. Silence.*] *Wonder what he's doing?* . . . You think he'll bring them back? Bunch of *whores!*

Kuvl. What?

Herbert. I said, *bunch of whores!* They're a bunch of common *whores!*

Kuvl. Why do you say that?

Herbert. What?

Kuvl. Why do you say they're *whores?* I'm . . . curious to know.

Herbert. Well, what *else* could they be? I mean just *look* at them. What else *could* they be? [*Long pause. And then, suddenly, the tapping starts again. Gradually it will build to fierce pounding.* Kuvl's *head sinks down onto the table.* HERBERT *spots the scattered building blocks. He rushes over.*] Maybe if I . . . try and . . . put these back together . . . *Do something good for a change.* Yes . . . [*He starts building with the blocks. It is, needless to say, not a very artistic effort, and bears no resemblance to the castle before it.*]

Old Gayve. I remember, I said to my son once, "Why do you sleep so much? When you're not at the Club you sleep *all the time.*" And you know what he said to me? . . . He said, "*Mind your own business.*" [OLD GAYVE *thinks about this, then laughs.*]

Ratscin. Gin.

Old Gayve. Hm?

Ratscin. Gin.

Old Gayve. Ahh. What luck, Ratscin. What *luck!* [*He slaps* RATSCIN *on the shoulder. And laughs.*]

Herbert [*staring up from the rubble*]. I don't remember what it looked like . . . [*He scatters the blocks.*] No. I'll build something else. [*He starts to gather them.*] What? . . . Build *what?* [*He scatters them.*] Oh, I'm no good at this. . . . [*He gets up from the floor and climbs back on his hobbyhorse.*]

Plaster from the ceiling falls on KUVL'S *head. He looks up in dismay. The pounding has begun to loosen the beams. The door opens and* RUDOLPH *staggers in, his clothes a mess. He manages to get to a chair. He collapses into it.*

Rudolph [*forcing a weak smile*]. I think I used the wrong approach. [*He points to the bottle of tequila.* KUVL *hands it to him. He takes a drink. He coughs. He spits it out.*] You *drink* that stuff?

Old Gayve. What happened, for God sakes!

Rudolph. I figured they were whores, you know? So . . . the first one I came to, I pinched on the ass. It was just a friendly gesture. Well, I guess she didn't see it that way. Neither did her friends. So. Guess they aren't whores. [*He groans and clutches his head.*] It's not easy getting hit over the head by eighteen tennis rackets. [*He laughs weakly.*]

Kuvl [pointing to an envelope in RUDOLPH'S *hand].*
What's that?

Rudolph. Oh. Yeah, they gave this to me. Said not to
open it till I got inside.

KUVL *takes it, tears it open, reads the scrap of paper it*
contained.

Ratscin. What's it say?

Kuvl. "Whores."

Long silence. HERBERT *tiptoes over to* RUDOLPH, *a smile*
on his face.

Herbert [to RUDOLPH, *sotto voce].* Thought you were
a big ladies' man. [*He giggles.*] Well, what happened?
Ladies' man.

RUDOLPH *looks up at* HERBERT. *A pause.*

Rudolph [to RATSCIN, *calmly.*] Hey. You know why
our Herbie here went beddy-bye on the front couch last
night? You know why he didn't go home?

Kuvl. Rudolph!

Rudolph. Huh? You know why?

Kuvl. Now look, *can* it, will you?

Rudolph. He didn't go home 'cause——

Kuvl. I said can it!

Rudolph. 'Cause——

Kuvl. Can it!

Rudolph. 'Cause his wife had already——

Kuvl. Now *look!*

Rudolph. Already——

Kuvl. Rudolph!!

Rudolph [calmly]. What? [*A pause.* KUVL *relaxes, the*
crisis passed.] Gonehomewithsomeoneelse.

HERBERT *nearly faints.*

Kuvl. Now *look*——

Herbert. That isn't true.

Kuvl. That isn't *true!*

Rudolph. Isn't *true* . . . ?

RUDOLPH *starts to laugh.* HERBERT *starts to cry.* KUVL
stares about in dismay.

Kuvl [*softly*]. It isn't true, Herbie. What he says . . . about Meryl . . . It isn't true. You know the way he talks.

Kuvl *looks back at* Rudolph. Rudolph *laughs, then stops, grips his side in pain. A beam descends from the ceiling. The house is falling apart.*

Ratscin [*to* Old Gayve]. You've given me too many cards. Pay attention to the game, will you?

Old Gayve. I'm sorry.

Old Gayve *mixes them up, starts to reshuffle. They play a while.* Kuvl *stares at his son and crumples the letter in his hand. Enter* Duncan, *in tennis outfit. He carries a racket.*

Duncan. Just wished to report, sir, that the wives and children have been spotted approaching the Club. They should be here in five minutes. Guests to follow. If all goes well. Ah, here we are. [*He picks a tennis ball up from the table and starts out.*]

Kuvl. What is that outfit you're wearing?

Duncan [*stopping*]. It's my tennis outfit. Don't you *like* it?

Kuvl. Like it? Of course I like it. It's mine.

Duncan. Yes, sir. I know. I got it out of your locker. Needed a little tapering. Had one of the maids do it. Hope you don't mind.

Kuvl. Mind? Why should I mind? Wouldn't want you to wear something that didn't *fit*.

Duncan. My sentiments exactly.

Kuvl. In fact, while we're at it, if there's anything *else* around the place you'd like, the furniture, the carpeting, please, don't hesitate—*steal* it.

Duncan. Yes, sir. Thank you. Very generous indeed. [*He starts to leave.*]

Kuvl. I'm just curious why you felt the need for my *tennis* outfit. That's all.

Duncan *stops.*

Duncan. Well, sir, you know, one can't very well play tennis in just *any* old thing.

Kuvl. Ah, I see. You're, um, off to play tennis.

Duncan. Yes, sir. The ladies have been so kind as to invite us to play. Well, we *told* them that none of us knew how. But they were most polite and said they'd *teach* us. Nice of them, don't you think?

Kuvl. Charming.

DUNCAN *smiles and goes to the door. He looks around.*

Duncan. Dusty in here, isn't it?   [*Leaves.*

Long pause. The plaster is now falling like snow. RATSCIN *and* OLD GAYVE *are valiantly playing cards.* RUDOLPH *is staring through a chink in the shutters. He has the bottle of tequila. He occasionally takes a drink.* HERBERT *is on his hobbyhorse. He is hugging the horse's neck.*

Old Gayve [*looking over his hand*]. Tsk-tsk-tsk-tsk-tsk-tsk-tsk . . . [*He broods, picks a card, and throws it.*]

Kuvl. So we're the committee. And what can we do? The telephone lines have been cut. Our wives and children are coming. The Happy Valley Country Club is due here at noon. (Today being guest day on top of it all.) And *what can we do?* . . . Nothing. [*A pause.*] I recall my father said to me once, "The president of this country club has a responsibility greater than the President of this country." And I remember I laughed at that remark. And he got angry. And explained *this* to me. . . . The President of a country, he said, has only two things to worry about—keeping his country prosperous, and keeping it from losing a war. But, he reasoned, it is highly unlikely that a country club, being self-sufficient, will *ever* become involved in a war. And as for prosperity, its membership is uncommonly rich. Therefore, he explained, the president of a country club has only one thing to worry about—keeping his country club *happy*. And, he said, as everyone knows, keeping people happy is *far* more difficult than either keeping them solvent, or keeping them alive. [*He laughs.*] From that lesson I learned that the relocation of sand traps, the hiring of top-name bands, and the employment of a really good chef . . . meant more than . . . anything. [*Long pause.*] So! My father founded this place. He and old Mr. Gayve. It was a large yellow swamp and they bought it cheap. And filled it in.

Then planted some trees. Some grass. Planted some flowers . . . *Built this house* . . . They had a *dream*, they said. [*He takes out a pair of spectacles, blows the dust off them.*] . . . I remember now. I had just turned thirty-one and was standing in the hallway, looking at the trophy cabinet. The windows were open. Funny. I can still remember the smell of the air. It was May. Like now. Only, I thing, not quite so cold. The flowers had all come out. So sweet it smelled. . . . [*Short pause.*] Then Herbert came running up. My father had died in his sleep. [*He puts on the glasses and looks about. The plaster keeps falling. He takes the glasses off.*] I don't need these glasses. Don't know why I use them. So. The clubhouse grew older. And *we* grew older in it. And as we did we guarded it from others; shared it with our friends. The bridle path. The pool. The fairways, the tennis courts. The *lake*. The *dance* hall! The *dining* hall (with its great floral curtains, its soft green walls). The steam room, too. Yes . . . and the gymnasium. The solarium! The movie theatre! The *bar!* [*Pause.*] *We spent our time here.* [*Pause.*] And we enjoyed ourselves. [*Pause.*] Then. Today these women came. These . . . strange women. . . . And cut the telephone wires. And disabled our cars. And took over our tennis courts. *Why?* [*Pause.*] Not to play tennis, *that's* for sure. [*Pause.*] Maybe if they hadn't cut the wires. [*He sighs.*] Well. So. Here we are. The committee. With nothing to do. And *that's* the crying shame of it. Nothing to do. [*He laughs silently.*] But sit in the Nursery like little children . . . and watch what we built collapse all about us.

The lights begin to fade.

Old Gayve [*looking through his hand*]. Tsk-tsk-tsk-tsk-tsk-tsk-tsk. [*He throws a card.* RATSCIN *picks it up.*] Gin?
    Ratscin. Not yet.
    Old Gayve [*barely audible*]. Tsk-tsk-tsk-tsk-tsk-tsk-tsk . . .
In the darkness the last sound that is heard is the sound of the tennis balls striking at the shutters. It continues for a while.

Slow curtain.